The Spread of
London's Underground

Capital Transport

Introduction

A cut and cover section of the Metropolitan Railway under construction at King's Cross and on the site of the original platforms, just east of the main line station which can be seen in the background. This is now the site of King's Cross Thameslink station.

By 1863, when the first part of the Underground was opened, most of the main line railways had built or were building their London terminal stations on the sites they occupy today. The Great Western, which had originally planned to share Euston station with the London & Birmingham Railway, instead opened their own station in 1854 at Paddington which was then a suburb in the west of London. Railways entering London from the south were barred from extending much further than the north bank of the Thames by the high cost of compensating landowners in the City of London. Lines from the east were able to reach the City's eastern boundary by demolishing and driving through poor housing districts. The wealth of the City was the magnet that the railway companies vied with each other to reach as carriers of goods as well as passengers. Because of the distance between the City and the terminal stations of the railways from the north and the west, road traffic connecting them to it and the emerging fashionable West End were clogging the thoroughfares.

The idea of a railway running entirely in tunnels beneath the streets came from a City solicitor, Charles Pearson, who set about persuading the public that his scheme was practicable. He managed to raise capital from the City of London as well as from the Great Western Railway, which was keen to have a rail connection with the City from its outlying terminus at Paddington, for the onward carriage from the west of passengers and freight, mainly meat and vegetables to feed the growing metropolis. The North Metropolitan Railway Company was therefore incorporated in 1853 to build a line from Edgware Road to King's Cross. In 1854 a Metropolitan Railway Act (that repealed the earlier one) authorised a line from Praed Street (and included a spur from the GWR at Bishops Road) to St Martin's le Grand (GPO) following the North Met route between Edgware Road and King's Cross. In 1859 St Martin's le Grand was

dropped in favour of a station at what was later called Farringdon Street, and the Praed Street terminus was dropped at the same time in favour of Bishops Road. Cut and cover construction was possible for most of the way between Paddington and King's Cross, since the route ran mainly beneath roads. At Farringdon Street space for a terminal became available by the removal of the City Cattle Market to Islington, which also allowed the City Corporation to erect a central meat market at Smithfield. The Great Western was quick to acquire the lease on its basement for its City goods depot which would be served by means of the new subterranean railway.

Initially, Great Western broad gauge trains provided the Metropolitan's service. The line was originally laid with broad gauge tracks of 7ft 0¼in and standard gauge tracks of 4ft 8½in, which enabled connecting standard gauge railways to reach their own City depots. This was to prove fortunate, since only six months after the opening of the line on 10 January 1863, the Great Western gave just one week's notice of its intention to withdraw its provision of

trains. The standard gauge Great Northern, through their junction to the west of King's Cross, filled the breach by loaning some of their engines and coaches to run the line until the Metropolitan Railway's own standard gauge trains were ready to take over the operation in 1867.

On 1 October 1863 GNR and GWR trains started running from their respective out of town stations, by way of the Metropolitan Railway's tracks, to terminate in the City. In 1867 the Metropolitan had more engines and carriages built to run a joint service with the GWR to Hammersmith and, by 1884, around the Circle Line.

This book shows, in diagrammatic map form, how London's Underground system developed from its beginning in 1863 until the close of the twentieth century. Each spread covers a ten year period. The maps on the right of each spread show the situation at the close of that decade. However, any developments during a particular decade that did not survive to its end and some that were planned but did not materialise until the following decade are also shown. Lines are colour coded in today's familiar hues, while station names and railway company nomenclature reflect that in use at the close of the span of each map. Punctuation within station names follows today's practice since its use on maps and signing has varied considerably over the years.

The text on each spread includes lists of stations opened, closed and any that changed their names within the decade. Within those lists, names in italics give the dates that stations were originally opened by railways that owned them before becoming part of the Underground network.

Thanks are due to Mike Horne who made available his invaluable database of station opening, re-naming and closure dates, and to A. J. Robertson, Brian Hardy and Peter Nichols who kindly checked the information contained in this book. Mike Harris carried out corrections for this second edition. A single map giving dates of all changes to the Underground network is Doug Rose's London Underground Diagrammatic History, recommended as complementary to the information within this book.

Second edition 2004
ISBN 185414 277 1

All photographs are copyright
London's Transport Museum, except:
pages 8, 10, 16 – commercial postcards
page 18 centre left and top right.
28, 30 – Capital Transport
page 20 left – B T Cooke
page 20 right – J H Meredith
page 22 bottom left – Colour Rail

Published by
Capital Transport Publishing,
P.O.Box 250, Harrow, Middlesex

Maps and text by Tim Demuth

Diagrammatic representations
of the London Underground network
and the New Johnston typeface are
© Transport for London

Printed by CS Graphics, Singapore

© Capital Transport Publishing 2004

Abbreviations of railway companies used in the text and on maps

A&BR	Aylesbury & Buckingham Railway 1868–1891		LNER	London & North Eastern Railway 1923–1947
BS&WR	Baker Street & Waterloo Railway (Bakerloo) 1906–1910		LNWR	London & North Western Railway 1846–1922
BR	British Railways / British Rail 1948–1996		LSWR	London & South Western Railway 1839–1922
CLR	Central London Railway 1900–1933		LPTB	London Passenger Transport Board 1933–1947
CCE&HR	Charing Cross Euston & Hampstead Railway 1907–1910		LT	London Transport 1933–2000
C&SLR	City & South London Railway 1890–1933		LTSR	London Tilbury & Southend Railway 1854–1920
DLR	Docklands Light Railway 1987–		MetR	Metropolitan Railway 1863–1933
ECR	Eastern Counties Railway 1839–1862		MDR	Metropolitan District Railway 1868–1933
ELR	East London Railway 1884–1947		Met&GCJt	Metropolitan & Great Central Joint Committee 1906–1947
GCR	Great Central Railway 1897–1922		MR	Midland Railway 1844–1922
GER	Great Eastern Railway 1862–1922		NLR	North London Railway 1853–1922
GNP&BR	Great Northern Piccadilly & Brompton Railway 1906–1910		O&AT	Oxford & Aylesbury Tramroad 1888–1899
GNR	Great Northern Railway 1848–1922		SECR	South Eastern & Chatham Railway 1899–1922
GW&GCJt	Great Western & Great Central Joint Committee 1899–1947		SER	South Eastern Railway 1843–1899
GWR	Great Western Railway 1838–1947		SR	Southern Railway 1923–1948
H&CR	Hammersmith & City Railway 1864–1867		W&CR	Waterloo & City Railway 1893–1907
LBSC	London Brighton & South Coast Railway 1840–1922		WLR	West London Railway 1844–1947
LCDR	London Chatham & Dover Railway 1859–1899		WLER	West London Extension Railway 1863–1947
LER	London Electric Railway 1910–1933		WT	Wotton Tramway 1871–1888
LMS	London Midland & Scottish Railway 1923–1947			

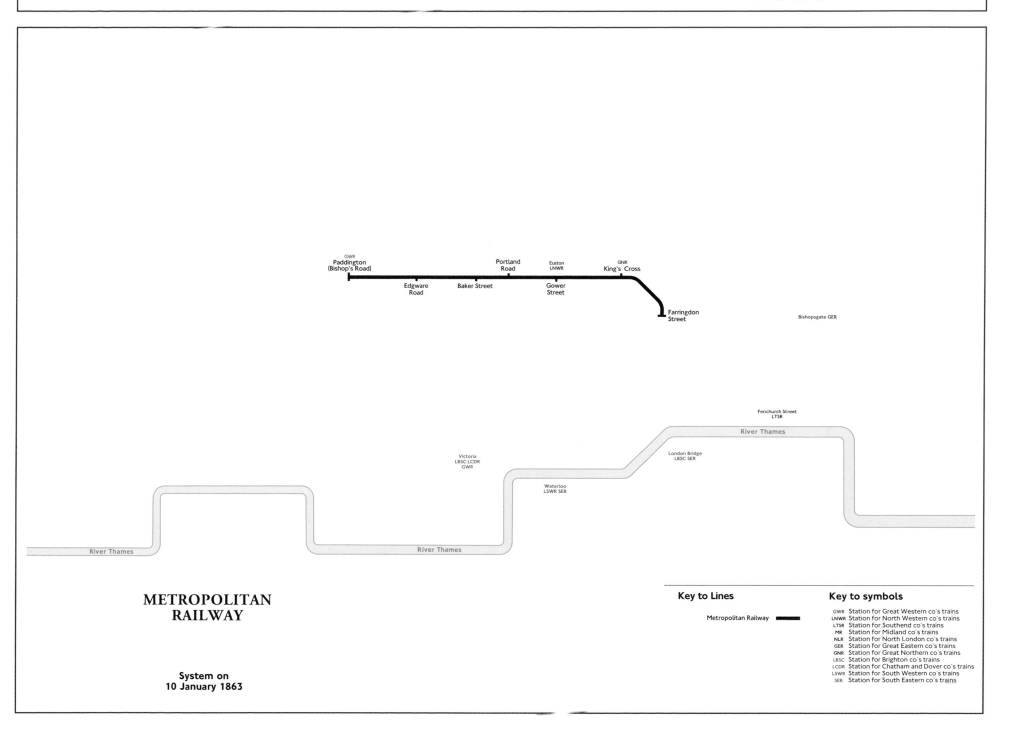

GWR
Paddington
(Bishop's Road)

Portland
Road

Euston
LNWR

GNR
King's Cross

Edgware
Road

Baker Street

Gower
Street

Farringdon
Street

Bishopsgate GER

Fenchurch Street
LTSR

River Thames

Victoria
LBSC LCDR
GWR

London Bridge
LBSC SER

Waterloo
LSWR SER

River Thames

River Thames

River Thames

METROPOLITAN
RAILWAY

System on
10 January 1863

Key to Lines

Metropolitan Railway ▬▬▬

Key to symbols

GWR Station for Great Western co's trains
LNWR Station for North Western co's trains
LTSR Station for Southend co's trains
MR Station for Midland co's trains
NLR Station for North London co's trains
GER Station for Great Eastern co's trains
GNR Station for Great Northern co's trains
LBSC Station for Brighton co's trains
LCDR Station for Chatham and Dover co's trains
LSWR Station for South Western co's trains
SER Station for South Eastern co's trains

Principal developments

1863 First section of the Metropolitan Railway opened between Paddington Bishop's Road and Farringdon with intermediate stations at Edgware Road, Baker Street, Portland Road (now Great Portland Street), Gower Street (Euston Square) and King's Cross on 10 January. It was worked by the Great Western Railway using their broad track gauge trains, until 10 August. From that date the GWR trains were replaced by standard track gauge trains hired from the Great Northern Railway until the Metropolitan Railway's own trains became available.

1863 Through GWR broad gauge service commenced between Farringdon Street, Paddington Bishop's Road and Windsor from 1 October.

1863 Junction constructed at King's Cross connecting Great Northern Railway with the Metropolitan Railway, enabling Great Northern trains to run into Farringdon Street, opened on 1 October.

1864 Hammersmith & City Railway is opened between Green Lane Junction (West-bourne Park) and Hammer-smith on 13 June, initially being worked by the Great Western Railway.

1865 Metropolitan Railway extended from Farringdon Street to Moorgate on 23 December.

1867 Formerly independent Hammersmith & City Railway

vested jointly with the Metropolitan and Great Western railways, being worked by the Metropolitan Railway from 1 July.

1868 Metropolitan & St John's Wood Railway opened between Baker Street and Swiss Cottage on 13 April.

1868 The Metropolitan Railway built a junction between Edgware Road and Paddington (Bishop's Road) allowing them to continue a line southwards through the fashionable district of Kensington, with stations at Paddington (Praed Street), Bayswater, Notting Hill Gate, Kensington (High Street) and Brompton (Gloucester Road). It opened on 1 October. The section from Gloucester Road to an end-on connection with the District Railway at South Kensington was opened on 24 December.

1868 The Metropolitan District Railway opened its first section between Westminster Bridge and South Kensington, with intermediate stations at St James's Park, Victoria (for the adjoining London Brighton & South Coast and London Chatham & Dover railways' terminal stations) and Sloane Square on 24 December, making an end-on junction with the Metropolitan's Kensington High Street branch.

1869 The East London Railway opened from New Cross LBSC (now New Cross Gate), through Brunel's Thames Tunnel (which had been adapted to take rails) to Wapping on 7 December. LBSC trains were provided.

1870 Metropolitan District Railway opens its line under the Victoria Embankment (which was constructed at the same time as part of the project) from Westminster to Blackfriars, with stations at Charing Cross and The Temple on 30 May.

Below A train of Metropolitan rolling stock using the standard gauge rails on the dual gauge H&CR at Hammersmith station.

These massive flyunders and bridges still survive to the west of Farringdon station. A GNR engine on the widened lines passes under a Metropolitan train heading for King's Cross, under the arch of Ray Street.

Opening dates of stations, name changes and closures

Stations opened or first served before 31.12.1862

20.06.1839	Stratford [ECR]
13.04.1854	Barking [LTSR]
22.08.1856	Buckhurst Hill [ECR]
22.08.1856	George Lane [ECR] *now South Woodford*
22.08.1856	Leytonstone [ECR]
22.08.1856	Loughton [ECR]
22.08.1856	Low Leyton [ECR] *now Leyton*
22.08.1856	Snaresbrook & Wanstead [ECR]
22.08.1856	Woodford [ECR]
31.03.1858	Bromley [LTSR] *now Bromley-by-Bow*
31.03.1858	East Ham [LTSR]
31.03.1858	Plaistow [LTSR]
2.06.1862	Kensington [WLR] *now Kensington (Olympia)*

Stations opened or first served after 1.01.1863

10.01.1863	Baker Street [H&C] MetR
10.01.1863	Edgware Road MetR
10.01.1863	Farringdon Street MetR *first site*
10.01.1863	Gower Street MetR *now Euston Square*
10.01.1863	King's Cross MetR *first site*
10.01.1863	Paddington (Bishop's Road) MetR
10.01.1863	Portland Road MetR *now Great Portland Street*
1.10.1863	Aylesbury [GWR]
13.06.1864	Hammersmith H&CR *first site*
13.06.1864	Notting Hill H&CR *now Ladbroke Grove*
13.06.1864	Shepherd's Bush H&CR
1.07.1864	Kensington [WLR] H&CR *first served*
24.04.1865	Blake Hall [GER]
24.04.1865	Chigwell Road [GER] *now Debden*
24.04.1865	Epping [GER]
24.04.1865	Loughton [GER] *present site*
24.04.1865	North Weald [GER]
24.04.1865	Ongar [GER] *Ongar*
24.04.1865	Theydon [GER] *now Theydon Bois*
23.12.1865	Aldersgate Street MetR *now Barbican*
23.12.1865	Farringdon Street MetR *present site*
23.12.1865	Moorgate Street MetR
1.02.1866	Westbourne Park & Kensal Green [GWR] H&CR *first site*
22.08.1867	East End, Finchley [GNR] *now East Finchley*
22.08.1867	Finchley & Hendon [GNR] *now Finchley Central*
22.08.1867	Mill Hill [GNR] *now Mill Hill East*
13.04.1868	Marlborough Road MetR
13.04.1868	St.John's Wood Road MetR
13.04.1868	Swiss Cottage MetR
23.09.1868	Grandborough Road [A&BR]
23.09.1868	Quainton Road [A&BR] *first site*
23.09.1868	Verney Junction [A&BR]
23.09.1868	Winslow Road [A&BR]
1.10.1868	Bayswater MetR
1.10.1868	Brompton (Gloucester Road) MetR
1.10.1868	Kensington (High Street) MetR
1.10.1868	Notting Hill Gate MetR
1.10.1868	Paddington (Praed Street) MetR
1.12.1868	Hammersmith H&CR *present site*
16.12.1868	Latimer Road H&CR
24.12.1868	St.James's Park MDR
24.12.1868	Sloane Square MDR
24.12.1868	South Kensington MetR
24.12.1868	Victoria MDR
24.12.1868	Westminster Bridge MDR
1.01.1869	Brentford Road [LSWR] *now Gunnersbury*
1.01.1869	Kew Gardens [LSWR]
1.01.1869	Hammersmith (Grove Road) [LSWR]
1.01.1869	Richmond [LSWR]
1.01.1869	Turnham Green [LSWR]
12.04.1869	Gloucester Road (Brompton) MDR
12.04.1869	West Brompton MDR
1.11.1869	Uxbridge Road [WLR] H&CR
7.12.1869	Deptford Road [ELR] *now Surrey Quays*
7.12.1869	New Cross LBSC [ELR] *now New Cross Gate*
7.12.1869	Rotherhithe [ELR]
7.12.1869	Wapping & Shadwell [ELR] *now Wapping*
30.05.1870	Blackfriars MDR
30.05.1870	Charing Cross MDR *now Embankment*
30.05.1870	The Temple MDR

Station names changed

	from	to
1.12.1865	Chigwell Road [GER]	Chigwell Lane
1.12.1865	Theydon [GER]	Theydon Bois
27.11.1867	Low Leyton [GER]	Leyton
1868	Kensington [WLR]	Kensington (Addison Road)
1869	Notting Hill [H&CR]	Notting Hill (Ladbroke Grove)
12.04.1869	Brompton (Gloucester Rd)	Gloucester Road (Brompton)

Stations last served by Underground trains

23.04.1865	Loughton [GER] *first site*
22.12.1865	Farringdon Street MetR *first site*
30.11.1868	Hammersmith H&CR *first site*

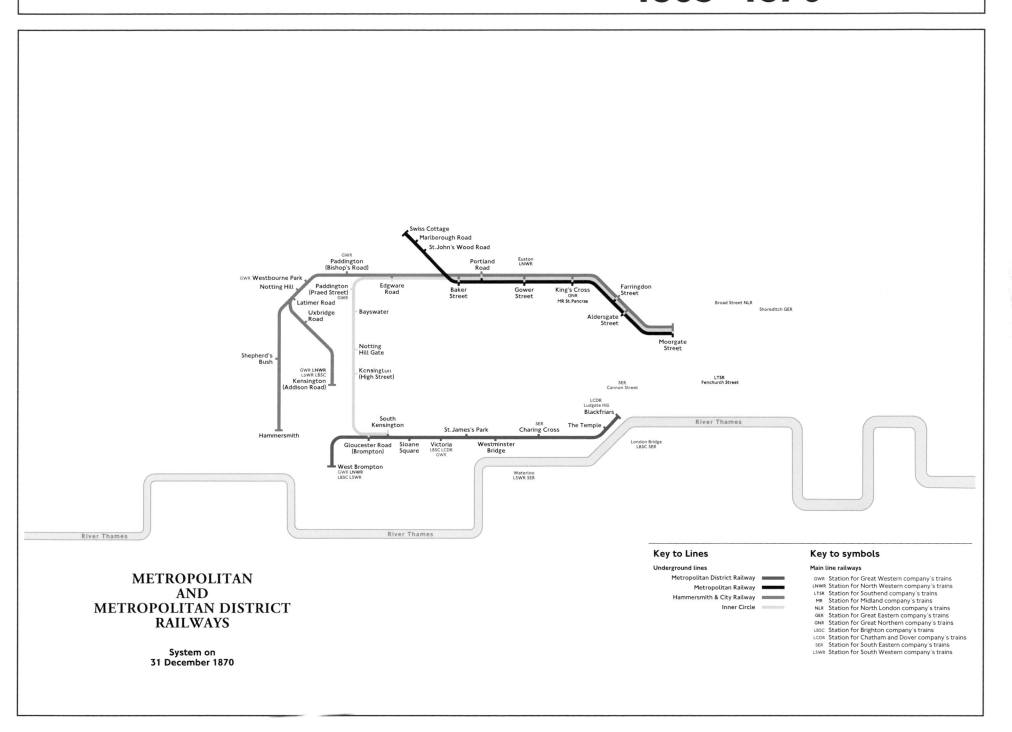

**METROPOLITAN
AND
METROPOLITAN DISTRICT
RAILWAYS**

**System on
31 December 1870**

Key to Lines

Underground lines

Metropolitan District Railway
Metropolitan Railway
Hammersmith & City Railway
Inner Circle

Key to symbols

Main line railways

GWR   Station for Great Western company's trains
LNWR   Station for North Western company's trains
LTSR   Station for Southend company's trains
MR   Station for Midland company's trains
NLR   Station for North London company's trains
GER   Station for Great Eastern company's trains
GNR   Station for Great Northern company's trains
LBSC   Station for Brighton company's trains
LCDR   Station for Chatham and Dover company's trains
SER   Station for South Eastern company's trains
LSWR   Station for South Western company's trains

Principal developments of the decade

1871 The first part of the Wotton Tramway, running through the Duke of Buckingham's private estate opened between Quainton Road and Wotton, on 1 April. The line was extended to its terminus at Brill a year later. It was later worked (but not owned) by the Metropolitan Railway.

1871 District Railway section between Blackfriars and Mansion House (which had its name altered from Cannon Street before the opening) opened 3 July.

1871 District Railway between High Street Kensington and Earl's Court opened 3 July.

1872 District Railway between Earl's Court and West Kensington opened 1 February.

1872 LNWR-operated Outer Circle service: Broad Street – Hampstead Heath – Willesden Junction – Kensington (Addison Road) – Earl's Court – Charing Cross – Mansion House, commenced 1 February.

1872 East London Railway between Wapping and Shoreditch, with a connection with the GER at Bishopsgate Junction, opened 10 April.

1872 GWR-operated Middle Circle service: Moorgate Street – Edgware Road – Paddington (Bishop's Road) – Latimer Road – Kensington (Addison Road) – Earl's Court – Charing Cross – Mansion House, commenced 1 July.

1874 District Railway between West Kensington and Hammersmith opened 9 September.

1875 Metropolitan Railway extended their line from Moorgate Street to Liverpool Street (GER terminus), where a junction was made with the Great Eastern Railway, on 1 February.

1875 The Metropolitan Railway opened Bishopsgate (the present Liverpool Street Circle Line station) on 12 July.

1876 Metropolitan Railway opened section between Bishopsgate and Aldgate on 18 November.

1877 Extension opened to Shaftesbury Road to connect MDR to LSWR route to Richmond, over which District Line trains have run ever since, on 1 June.

1878 Subway constructed to take Hammersmith & City tracks under the GWR main line between Royal Oak and Westbourne Park stations.

1879 MDR section between Turnham Green and Ealing Broadway station adjacent to that of the GWR, opened 1 July.

1879 Metropolitan Railway trains ran over the Metropolitan & St John's Wood Railway between Swiss Cottage and West Hampstead from 30 June.

1879 MetR trains ran over the Met&SJWR between West Hampstead to Willesden Green from 24 November.

1880 MDR between West Brompton and Putney Bridge opened 1 March.

1880 ELR between Deptford Road (now Surrey Quays) and New Cross (SER) opened 1 April.

1880 MetR trains ran over the Met&SJWR between Willesden Green and Harrow-on-the-Hill from 2 August.

Junctions underground were more complicated than outside by having to avoid the uprights supporting the ceiling. This is the scene on the Metropolitan District Railway, with Mansion House station in the distance, in the mid-1870s.

Opening dates of stations, name changes and closures

Stations opened or first served

1.04.1871	Waddesdon [WT]	
1.04.1871	Westcott [WT]	
1.04.1871	Wotton [WT]	
3.07.1871	Kensington (High Street)	MDR
3.07.1871	Mansion House	MDR
30.10.1871	Royal Oak	H&CR
30.10.1871	Earl's Court	MDR *first site*
30.10.1871	Westbourne Park	H&CR *present site*
01.1872	Wood Siding [WT]	
04.1872	Brill [WT]	
1.04.1872	High Barnet [GNR]	
1.04.1872	Torrington Park, Woodside [GNR] *now Woodside Park*	
1.04.1872	Totteridge [GNR] *now Totteridge & Whetstone*	
1.04.1873	Shaftesbury Road [LSWR] *now Ravenscourt Park*	
9.09.1874	Hammersmith	MDR
9.09.1874	North End (Fulham)	MDR *now West Kensington*
1.02.1875	Liverpool Street [GER]	MetR
12.07.1875	Bishopsgate	MetR *now Liverpool Street*
10.04.1876	Shadwell [ELR]	
10.04.1876	Shoreditch [ELR]	
10.04.1876	Whitechapel [ELR]	
18.11.1876	Aldgate	MetR
1.06.1877	Gunnersbury [LSWR]	MDR
1.06.1877	Kew Gardens [LSWR]	MDR
1.06.1877	Richmond (New Station) [LSWR]	MDR
1.06.1877	Shaftesbury Road [LSWR]	MDR *now Ravenscourt Park*
1.06.1877	Turnham Green [LSWR]	MDR
1.10.1877	Hammersmith (Grove Road) [LSWR]	H&CR
1.02.1878	Earl's Court	MDR *present site*
30.06.1879	Finchley Road	MetR
30.06.1879	West Hampstead	MetR
1.07.1879	Acton Green	MDR *now Chiswick Park*
1.07.1879	Ealing Broadway	MDR
1.07.1879	Ealing Common	MDR
1.07.1879	Mill Hill Park	MDR *now Acton Town*
24.11.1879	Kilburn & Brondesbury	MetR *now Kilburn*
24.11.1879	Willesden Green	MetR
1.03.1880	Parsons Green	MDR
1.03.1880	Putney Bridge & Fulham	MDR *now Putney Bridge*
1.03.1880	Walham Green	MDR *now Fulham Broadway*
2.08.1880	Harrow	MetR *now Harrow-on-the-Hill*
2.08.1880	Kingsbury & Neasden	MetR *now Neasden*

Station names changed

	from	to
1.11.1871	Brentford Road [LSWR]	Gunnersbury
1.02.1872	Finchley & Hendon [GNR]	Finchley
1.04.1874	Totteridge [GNR]	Totteridge & Whetstone
10.04.1876	Wapping & Shadwell	Wapping
1.03.1877	North End (Fulham)	West Kensington
c.1879	Kensington (High Street)	High Street Kensington
1880	Notting Hill (Ladbroke Grove)	Notting Hill & Ladbroke Grove

Stations last served by Underground trains

29.10.1871	Westbourne Park	MetR *first site*
11.07.1875	Liverpool Street [GER]	*first station*
31.01.1878	Earl's Court	MDR *first station*

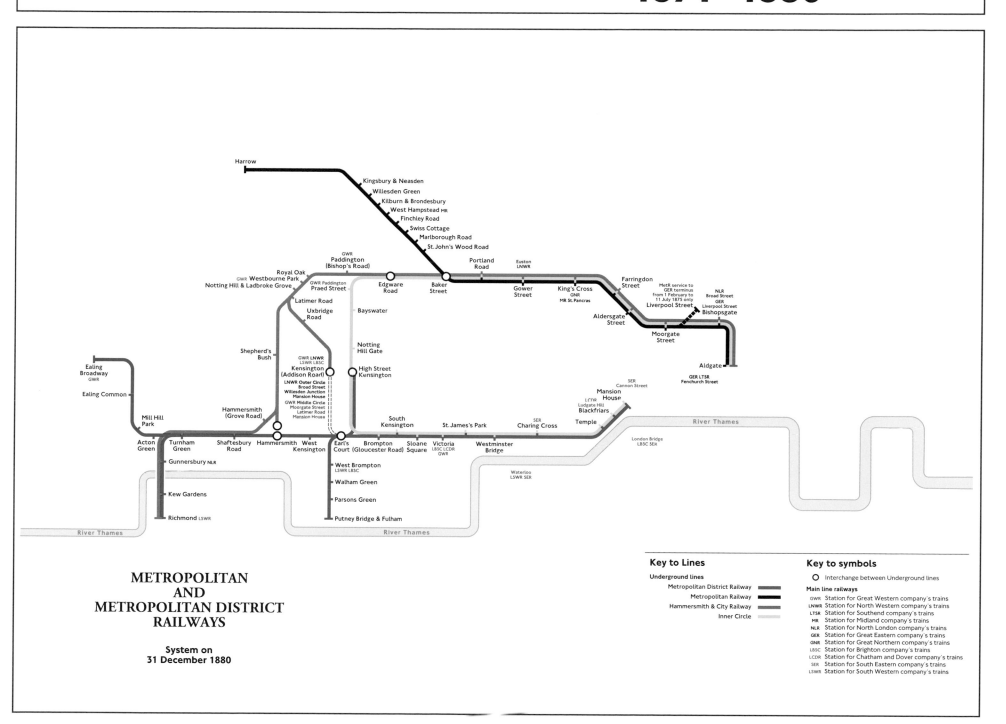

Harrow

Kingsbury & Neasden
Willesden Green
Kilburn & Brondesbury
West Hampstead MR
Finchley Road
Swiss Cottage
Marlborough Road
St. John's Wood Road

GWR
Paddington
(Bishop's Road)

Portland
Road

Euston
LNWR

Royal Oak
GWR Westbourne Park
Notting Hill & Ladbroke Grove

GWR Paddington
Praed Street

Edgware
Road

Baker
Street

Gower
Street

King's Cross
GNR
MR St.Pancras

Farringdon
Street

MetR service to
GER terminus
from 1 February to
11 July 1875 only
Liverpool Street

NLR
Broad Street
GER
Liverpool Street
Bishopsgate

Latimer Road

Uxbridge
Road

Bayswater

Aldersgate
Street

Shepherd's
Bush

GWR LNWR
LSWR LBSC
Kensington
(Addison Road)

Notting
Hill Gate

High Street
Kensington

Moorgate
Street

Aldgate

Ealing
Broadway
GWR

LNWR Outer Circle
Broad Street
Willesden Junction
Mansion House
GWR Middle Circle
Moorgate Street
Latimer Road
Mansion House

GER LTSR
Fenchurch Street

Ealing Common

SER
Cannon Street

Mansion
House

Mill Hill
Park

Hammersmith
(Grove Road)

South
Kensington

St. James's Park

SER
Charing Cross

LCDR
Ludgate Hill
Blackfriars

Temple

River Thames

Acton
Green

Turnham
Green

Shaftesbury
Road

Hammersmith

West
Kensington

Earl's
Court (Gloucester Road)

Brompton

Sloane
Square

Victoria
LBSC LCDR
GWR

Westminster
Bridge

London Bridge
LBSC SER

Gunnersbury NLR

West Brompton
LSWR LBSC

Waterloo
LSWR SER

Kew Gardens

Walham Green

Richmond LSWR

Parsons Green

River Thames

Putney Bridge & Fulham

River Thames

METROPOLITAN AND METROPOLITAN DISTRICT RAILWAYS

System on 31 December 1880

Key to Lines

Underground lines

Metropolitan District Railway
Metropolitan Railway
Hammersmith & City Railway
Inner Circle

Key to symbols

○ Interchange between Underground lines

Main line railways

GWR   Station for Great Western company's trains
LNWR   Station for North Western company's trains
LTSR   Station for Southend company's trains
MR   Station for Midland company's trains
NLR   Station for North London company's trains
GER   Station for Great Eastern company's trains
GNR   Station for Great Northern company's trains
LBSC   Station for Brighton company's trains
LCDR   Station for Chatham and Dover company's trains
SER   Station for South Eastern company's trains
LSWR   Station for South Western company's trains

Principal developments of the decade

Below Cover of a large fold-out map of the District Railway published in the year of Queen Victoria's golden jubilee.

1882 Ownership of the Metropolitan & St John's Wood Railway was passed to the Metropolitan Railway on 3 July.

1882 Metropolitan Railway extended the future Inner Circle from Aldgate to Tower of London (now Tower Hill), which opened on 25 September.

1883 District Railway started running its own trains between Mansion House, Ealing Broadway GWR and Windsor GWR, from 1 March.

1883 MDR opened line between Mill Hill Park (now Acton Town) and Hounslow (later Hounslow Town) on 1 May.

1884 MDR opened direct line to Hounslow Barracks on 21 July, leaving Hounslow Town as the terminus of a branch.

1884 St Mary's, owned jointly by the MDR and MetR, and the connection to the ELR, opened on 3 March for SER trains.

1884 First Metropolitan and District services over the East London Railway from St Mary's to New Cross (SER) (MetR trains) and New Cross (ELR) – adjacent to New Cross (LBSC) (MDR trains) on 1 October. From that date the ELR was leased jointly by the MDR and MetR as well as the LBSC, LCDR, SER, and later the GER.

1884 The link which completed the Inner Circle opened between Mansion House and Mark Lane on 6 October and was vested jointly with the Metropolitan District and Metropolitan railways. Mark Lane to Whitechapel also opened on 6 October. Intermediate stations were at Cannon Street and Eastcheap (later The Monument). The clockwise service was run by Metropolitan Railway trains, the anti-clockwise service by District Railway trains, plus a few MetR trains; a proportion to reflect the larger MetR owned mileage.

1885 Harrow to Pinner opened on 25 May.

1885 The MDR suspends Windsor service in favour of the faster and more comfortable GWR trains on 30 September.

1886 Branch to Hounslow Town closed on 31 March.

1887 Pinner to Rickmansworth opened on 1 September.

1889 District Railway trains commence running over the LSWR-owned line from the River Thames bridge at Putney to Wimbledon, from 3 June.

1889 Rickmansworth to Chesham opened on 8 July.

1890 London's first deep level tube railway, the City & South London Railway, opened between King William Street and Stockwell on 18 December. Using electric locomotives hauling carriages, the trains ran through tunnels bored through London's clay and deep enough for stations to require lifts between platforms and ground level.

When the District Railway worked its own system it had 24 engines built in 1871, which were similar to those already in use by the Metropolitan Railway. It ordered more in 1876, 1880, 1883, 1884 and 1886, bringing the total to 54, to go with its 4-wheeled compartment coaches, all of which lasted until the end of steam on the District early in the twentieth century. This type of train also provided the short-lived service from Mansion House to Windsor which ran from 1 March 1883 to 30 September 1885, but was no match for the GWR 8-wheeled carriages running smoothly on broad gauge tracks behind powerful engines.

Opening dates of stations, name changes and closures

Stations opened or first served by Underground trains

Date	Station	Notes
25.09.1882	Tower of London MDR MetR	*on site of present Tower Hill*
1.03.1883	Castle Hill (Ealing Dean) [GWR] MDR	
1.03.1883	Ealing Broadway [GWR] MDR	
1.03.1883	Hanwell [GWR] MDR	
1.03.1883	Hayes [GWR] MDR	
1.03.1883	Langley [GWR] MDR	
1.03.1883	Slough [GWR] MDR *first site*	
1.03.1883	Southall [GWR] MDR	
1.03.1883	West Drayton [GWR] MDR *first site*	
1.03.1883	Windsor [GWR] MDR	
1.05.1883	Boston Road MDR *now Boston Manor*	
1.05.1883	Hounslow MDR *original site*	
1.05.1883	Osterley & Spring Grove MDR *first site*	
1.05.1883	South Ealing MDR	
21.07.1884	Hounslow Barracks MDR	*now Hounslow West*
9.08.1884	West Drayton [GWR] MDR *present site*	
8.09.1884	Slough [GWR] MDR *present site*	
1.10.1884	Deptford Road [ELR] MDR MetR	
1.10.1884	New Cross LBSC [ELR] MDR *first site*	
1.10.1884	New Cross SER [ELR] MetR	
1.10.1884	Rotherhithe [ELR] MDR MetR	
1.10.1884	St.Mary's MDR MetR	
1.10.1884	Shadwell [ELR] MDR MetR	
1.10.1884	Wapping [ELR] MDR MetR	
6.10.1884	Aldgate East MDR MetR *first site*	
6.10.1884	Cannon Street MDR MetR	
6.10.1884	Eastcheap MDR MetR *now Monument*	
6.10.1884	Mark Lane MDR MetR *first site*	
6.10.1884	Whitechapel (Mile End) MDR	
25.05.1885	Pinner MetR	
1.04.1886	Heston-Hounslow MDR	*now Hounslow Central*
1.09.1886	New Cross LBSC [ELR] MDR *second site*	
1.09.1887	Northwood MetR	
1.09.1887	Rickmansworth MetR	
3.06.1889	East Putney [LSWR] MDR	
3.06.1889	Southfields [LSWR] MDR	
3.06.1889	Wimbledon [LSWR] MDR	
3.06.1889	Wimbledon Park [LSWR] MDR	
8.07.1889	Chesham MetR	
8.07.1889	Chalfont Road MetR	*now Chalfont & Latimer*
8.07.1889	Chorley Wood MetR	
18.12.1890	Borough C&SLR	
18.12.1890	Elephant & Castle C&SLR	
18.12.1890	Kennington C&SLR	
18.12.1890	King William Street C&SLR	
18.12.1890	The Oval C&SLR	
18.12.1890	Stockwell C&SLR	

Station names changed

Date	from	to
1.05.1882	Torrington Park, Woodside [GNR]	Woodside Park [GNR]
21.07.1884	Hounslow	Hounslow Town
1.11.1884	Eastcheap	The Monument
11.09.1885	Finchley Road	Finchley Road (South Hampstead)
1886	Ealing Common	Ealing Common & West Acton
1.02.1887	*East End, Finchley [GNR]*	*East Finchley*
03.1887	Acton Green	Chiswick Park & Acton Green
1.03.1888	Shaftesbury Road	Ravenscourt Park

Stations last served by Underground trains

Date	Station	Notes
8.08.1884	West Drayton [GWR] MDR *first station*	
7.09.1884	Slough [GWR] MDR *first station*	
12.10.1884	Tower of London MDR MetR	
30.09.1885	Castle Hill (Ealing Dean) [GWR] MDR	
30.09.1885	Ealing Broadway [GWR]) MDR	
30.09.1885	Hanwell [GWR] MDR	
30.09.1885	Hayes [GWR] MDR	
30.09.1885	Langley [GWR] MDR	
30.09.1885	Slough [GWR] MDR *second station*	
30.09.1885	Southall [GWR] MDR	
30.09.1885	West Drayton [GWR] MDR *second station*	
30.09.1885	Windsor [GWR] MDR	
31.3.1886	Hounslow Town MDR	
31.8.1886	New Cross LBSC [ELR] MDR *first site*	

Jubilee Edition of the District Railway Map of London 1887. Mounted Copy 1/6 or with Case 2/c. Price 1/6. W.J.Adams & Sons, Bradshaw's Guide Office. 59 Fleet Street, London, E.C.

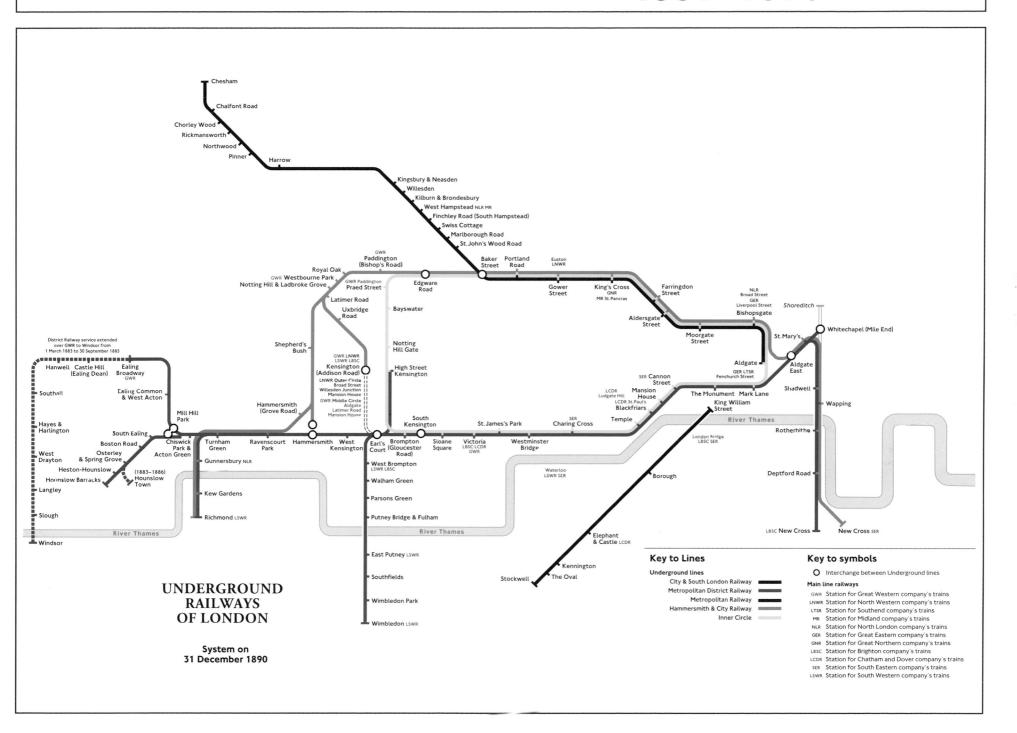

Chesham

Chalfont Road

Chorley Wood

Rickmansworth

Northwood

Pinner

Harrow

Kingsbury & Neasden

Willesden

Kilburn & Brondesbury

West Hampstead NLR MR

Finchley Road (South Hampstead)

Swiss Cottage

Marlborough Road

St. John's Wood Road

GWR
Paddington
(Bishop's Road)

Baker Street

Portland Road

Euston
LNWR

Gower Street

King's Cross
GNR
MR St.Pancras

Farringdon Street

NLR
Broad Street
GER
Liverpool Street
Bishopsgate

Shoreditch

Whitechapel (Mile End)

Royal Oak

GWR Westbourne Park

Notting Hill & Ladbroke Grove

GWR Paddington
Praed Street

Edgware Road

Latimer Road

Uxbridge Road

Bayswater

Aldersgate Street

Moorgate Street

St. Mary's

Shepherd's Bush

GWR LNWR
LSWR LBSC
Kensington
(Addison Road)
LNWR Outer Circle
Broad Street
Willesden Junction
Mansion House
GWR Middle Circle
Aldgate
Latimer Road
Mansion House

Notting Hill Gate

High Street Kensington

Aldgate
GER LTSR
Fenchurch Street

Aldgate East

Shadwell

District Railway service extended
over GWR to Windsor from
1 March 1883 to 30 September 1885

Hanwell   Castle Hill
(Ealing Dean)

Ealing
Broadway
GWR

SER Cannon Street

Mansion House
LCDR St.Paul's
Blackfriars

The Monument   Mark Lane

Wapping

Southall

Ealing Common
& West Acton

LCDR
Ludgate Hill

Hammersmith
(Grove Road)

King William Street

Hayes &
Harlington

Mill Hill Park

South Kensington

St. James's Park

SER
Charing Cross

Temple

River Thames

Rotherhithe

South Ealing

Chiswick
Park &
Acton Green

Turnham Green

Ravenscourt Park

Hammersmith   West Kensington

Earl's Court

Bromption
(Gloucester Road)

Sloane Square

Victoria
LBSC LCDR
GWR

Westminster Bridge

London Bridge
LBSC SER

West
Drayton

Boston Road

Osterley
& Spring Grove

Gunnersbury NLR

West Brompton
LSWR LBSC

Deptford Road

Heston-Hounslow

(1883–1886)
Hounslow
Town

Hounslow Barracks

Walham Green

Waterloo
LSWR SER

Borough

Langley

Kew Gardens

Parsons Green

Slough

Richmond LSWR

Putney Bridge & Fulham

LBSC New Cross

New Cross SER

Windsor

River Thames

River Thames

Elephant
& Castle LCDR

East Putney LSWR

UNDERGROUND
RAILWAYS
OF LONDON

Southfields

Kennington

Stockwell

The Oval

**System on
31 December 1890**

Wimbledon Park

Wimbledon LSWR

Key to Lines

Underground lines

City & South London Railway	▬▬▬
Metropolitan District Railway	▬▬▬
Metropolitan Railway	▬▬▬
Hammersmith & City Railway	▬▬▬
Inner Circle	▬▬▬

Key to symbols

◯ Interchange between Underground lines

Main line railways

GWR Station for Great Western company's trains
LNWR Station for North Western company's trains
LTSR Station for Southend company's trains
MR Station for Midland company's trains
NLR Station for North London company's trains
GER Station for Great Eastern company's trains
GNR Station for Great Northern company's trains
LBSC Station for Brighton company's trains
LCDR Station for Chatham and Dover company's trains
SER Station for South Eastern company's trains
LSWR Station for South Western company's trains

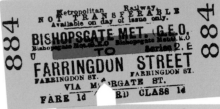

Principal developments of the decade

Central London Railway

1900 Opening of Central London Railway between Shepherd's Bush and Bank, with intermediate stations at Holland Park, Notting Hill Gate, Queen's Road, Lancaster Gate, Marble Arch, Oxford Circus, Tottenham Court Road, British Museum, Chancery Lane and Post Office, on 30 July. Bond Street opened on 24 September.

City & South London Railway

1900 City & South London Railway opened the section between Borough and Moorgate Street, with stations at London Bridge and Bank and closed their original City terminus at King William Street, on 25 February.

1900 Extension from Stockwell to Clapham Common with an intermediate station at Clapham Road (now Clapham North) opened on 3 June.

Metropolitan Railway

1891 Aylesbury & Buckingham Railway absorbed by Metropolitan Railway, 1 July.

1892 The line opened between Chalfont Road and Aylesbury South Junction, with intermediate stations at Amersham, Great Missenden, Wendover and Stoke Mandeville, on 1 September.

1894 Aylesbury South Junction connected to North Junction and to the Metropolitan Railway's newly absorbed Aylesbury to Verney Junction section, on 1 January.

1899 Working of the Quainton Road to Brill Oxford & Aylesbury Tramroad was taken over by the Metropolitan Railway on 1 December. Ownership of the trackbed remained with the Trustees of the late Earl Temple's Estate.

Metropolitan and District Railways

1900 While both railways accept the need and urgency to electrify the Inner Circle line, neither could agree as to the system to be employed. The Metropolitan Railway favoured high voltage 3-phase alternating current, collected from two overhead wires. The District Railway wished to proceed with the direct current third rail system, already used by the City & South London and Central London tubes, the Liverpool Overhead Railway, numerous American cities and by metropolitan railways in Berlin, Paris and Budapest (home of Ganz & Co, the manufacturers of the Metropolitan Railway's preferred 3-phase equipment). A Board of Trade arbitration commission, which was set up on 29 October, reported on 15 November in favour of the direct current system proposed by the District Railway, where the current was picked up from a rail laid outside the running rails and returned to a rail between them, which remains standard throughout the Underground today.

Waterloo & City Railway

1898 Waterloo & City Railway opened on 8 August.

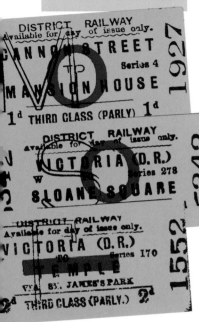

Ticket security Is not new. At the end of the nineteenth century the District and Metropolitan railways were printing various devices on their tickets to help ease checking. On Inner Circle tickets the red 'O' in the centre referred to clockwise travel on the Outer rail. Conversely, a red 'I' indicated anti-clockwise journeys on the Inner rail. Large outline letters were intended to help ticket collectors at barriers identify their own stations.

The Central London Railway opened using electric locomotives hauling trains of carriages, as had the City & South London Railway when it opened ten years earlier. But the CLR's engines were heavier and more powerful, causing vibration to the driver as well as to occupants of buildings above the line. It can be seen here how the driver was accommodated within the massive steel frames of the locomotive.

C.L.R. Twopenny Tube.
The Train.

Opening dates of stations, name changes and closures

Stations opened or first served by Underground trains

1.07.1891	Grandborough Road	MetR *opened by A&BR 23.09.1868*
1.07.1891	Quainton Road	MetR *opened by A&BR 23.09.1868*
1.07.1891	Verney Junction	MetR *opened by A&BR 23.09.1868*
1.07.1891	Winslow Road	MetR *opened by A&BR 23.09.1868*
1.09.1892	Amersham	MetR
1.09.1892	Aylesbury	MetR *first site*
1.09.1892	Great Missenden	MetR
1.09.1892	Stoke Mandeville	MetR
1.09.1892	Wendover	MetR
1.01.1894	Aylesbury	MetR *present site*
12.05.1894	Wembley Park	MetR
30.11.1896	Quainton Road	MetR *present site*
1.01.1897	Waddesdon Manor	MetR *later Waddesdon*
8.08.1898	City	[W&CR]
8.08.1898	Waterloo	[W&CR]
1.12.1899	Brill	[O&AT] MetR *opened by WT 06.1872*
1.12.1899	Waddesdon Road	[O&AT] MetR *opened by WT 1.04.1871*
1.12.1899	Westcott	[O&AT] MetR *opened by WT 1.04.1871*
1.12.1899	Wood Siding	[O&AT] MetR *opened by WT 06.1871*
1.12.1899	Wotton	[O&AT] MetR *opened by WT 1.04.1871*
25.02.1900	Bank	C&SLR
25.02.1900	London Bridge	C&SLR
25.02.1900	Moorgate Street	C&SLR *now Moorgate*
3.06.1900	Clapham Common	C&SLR
3.06.1900	Clapham Road	C&SLR *now Clapham North*
30.07.1900	Bank	CLR
30.07.1900	British Museum	CLR
30.07.1900	Chancery Lane	CLR
30.07.1900	Holland Park	CLR
30.07.1900	Lancaster Gate	CLR
30.07.1900	Marble Arch	CLR
30.07.1900	Notting Hill Gate	CLR
30.07.1900	Oxford Circus	CLR
30.07.1900	Post Office	CLR
30.07.1900	Queen's Road	CLR *now Queensway*
30.07.1900	Shepherd's Bush	CLR
30.07.1900	Tottenham Court Road	CLR
24.09.1900	Bond Street	CLR

Station names changed

	from	to
1892	Turnham Green	Turnham Green (Bedford Park)
1894	The Oval	Oval
1.06.1894	Harrow	Harrow-on-the-Hill
1.06.1894	Willesden Green	Willesden Green & Cricklewood
1.07.1900	Shadwell	Shadwell & St.George-in-the-East

Stations last served by Underground trains

31.12.1893	Aylesbury	*first site*
29.11.1896	Quainton Road	*first site*
24.02.1900	King William Street	C&SLR

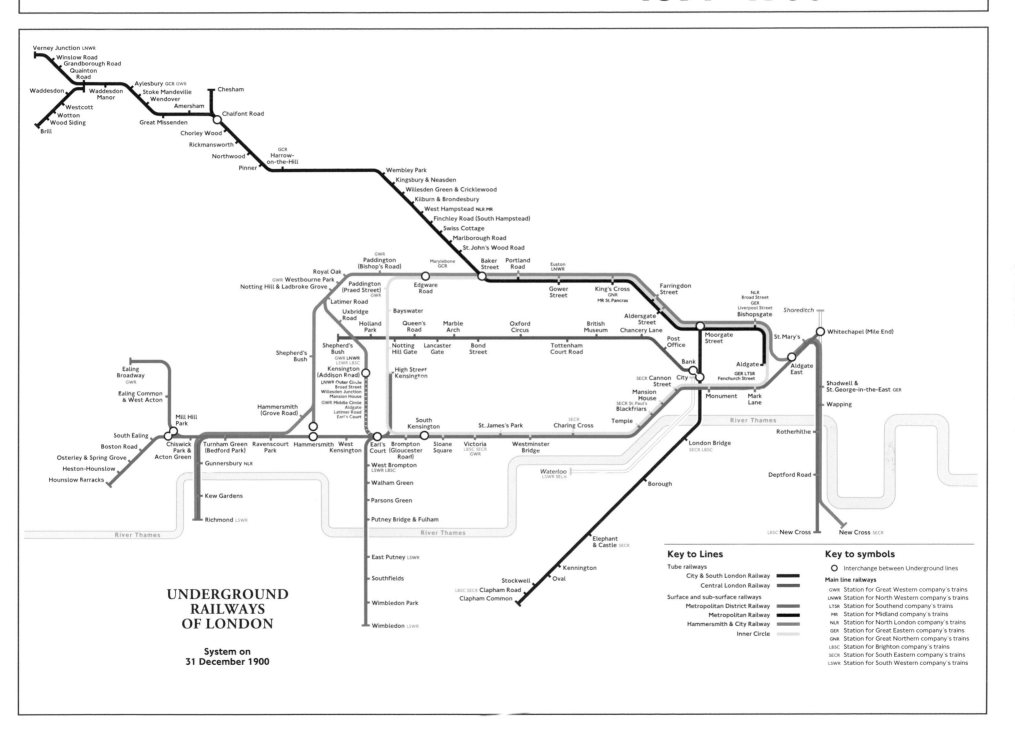

Verney Junction LNWR
Winslow Road
Grandborough Road
Quainton Road
Waddesdon
Aylesbury GCR GWR
Waddesdon Manor
Stoke Mandeville
Wendover
Amersham
Chesham
Westcott
Wotton
Wood Siding
Great Missenden
Chalfont Road
Brill
Chorley Wood
Rickmansworth
GCR Harrow-on-the-Hill
Northwood
Pinner
Wembley Park
Kingsbury & Neasden
Willesden Green & Cricklewood
Kilburn & Brondesbury
West Hampstead NLR MR
Finchley Road (South Hampstead)
Swiss Cottage
Marlborough Road
St. John's Wood Road

GWR Paddington (Bishop's Road)
Marylebone GCR
Baker Street
Portland Road
Euston LNWR
Royal Oak
GWR Westbourne Park
Notting Hill & Ladbroke Grove
Paddington (Praed Street) GWR
Edgware Road
Gower Street
King's Cross GNR MR St. Pancras
Farringdon Street
NLR Broad Street GER Liverpool Street Bishopsgate
Latimer Road
Uxbridge Road
Holland Park
Bayswater
Queen's Road
Marble Arch
Oxford Circus
British Museum
Aldersgate Street
Chancery Lane
Shoreditch
Whitechapel (Mile End)
Shepherd's Bush
Shepherd's Bush GWR LNWR LSWR LBSC
Notting Hill Gate
Lancaster Gate
Bond Street
Tottenham Court Road
Post Office
Moorgate Street
St. Mary's
Ealing Broadway GWR
Kensington (Addison Road)
High Street Kensington
Bank
Aldgate
Aldgate East
Ealing Common & West Acton
LNWR Outer Circle Broad Street Willesden Junction Mansion House GWR Middle Circle Aldgate Latimer Road Earl's Court
City
GER LTSR Fenchurch Street
Shadwell & St. George-in-the-East GER
Hammersmith (Grove Road)
SECR Cannon Street
Mansion House
Monument
Mark Lane
Wapping
Mill Hill Park
South Kensington
St. James's Park
SECR St. Paul's Blackfriars
Temple
River Thames
Rotherhithe
South Ealing
Boston Road
Chiswick Park & Acton Green
Turnham Green (Bedford Park)
Ravenscourt Park
Hammersmith
West Kensington
Earl's Court
Brompton (Gloucester Road)
Sloane Square
Victoria LBSC SECR GWR
Westminster Bridge
London Bridge SECR LBSC
Osterley & Spring Grove
Gunnersbury NLR
West Brompton LSWR LBSC
SECR Charing Cross
Heston-Hounslow
Hounslow Barracks
Waterloo LSWR SECR
Borough
Deptford Road
Kew Gardens
Walham Green
Richmond LSWR
Parsons Green
Putney Bridge & Fulham
River Thames
River Thames
Elephant & Castle SECR
LBSC New Cross
New Cross SECR
East Putney LSWR
Kennington
Southfields
Stockwell
Oval
LBSC SECR Clapham Road
Wimbledon Park
Clapham Common
Wimbledon LSWR

UNDERGROUND RAILWAYS OF LONDON

System on 31 December 1900

Key to Lines
Tube railways
City & South London Railway
Central London Railway
Surface and sub-surface railways
Metropolitan District Railway
Metropolitan Railway
Hammersmith & City Railway
Inner Circle

Key to symbols
○ Interchange between Underground lines
Main line railways
GWR Station for Great Western company's trains
LNWR Station for North Western company's trains
LTSR Station for Southend company's trains
MR Station for Midland company's trains
NLR Station for North London company's trains
GER Station for Great Eastern company's trains
GNR Station for Great Northern company's trains
LBSC Station for Brighton company's trains
SECR Station for South Eastern company's trains
LSWR Station for South Western company's trains

UNDERGROUND
DISTRICT RAILWAY.
Issued subject to the Companies' Bye Laws, Rules, Regulations and advertised Conditions.

8779

Mansion House
S.76   TO   S.76
VICTORIA
or any intermediate Station.
ORDINARY CAR (3rd Class) FARE **2d.**
Available on day of issue only.

London & South Western Ry.
RICHMOND NEW to
KEW GARDENS

Richmond New to Kew Gardens	Richmond New to Kew Gardens
THIRD CLASS	THIRD CLASS
(S.152) See over	
Fare 1d	Fare 1d

840

Principal developments of the decade

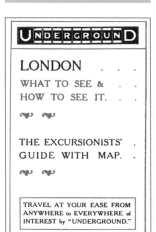

UNDERGROUND

LONDON . . .
WHAT TO SEE & . .
HOW TO SEE IT. . .

ᴦᴕ   ᴦᴕ

THE EXCURSIONISTS'
GUIDE WITH MAP. .

ᴦᴕ   ᴦᴕ

TRAVEL AT YOUR EASE FROM
ANYWHERE to EVERYWHERE of
INTEREST by "UNDERGROUND."

Baker Street & Waterloo Railway

1906 Opening of line, Baker Street to Kennington Road, on 10 March.

1906 Extension to Elephant & Castle on 5 August.

1907 Baker Street to Great Central opened on 27 March.

1907 Great Central to Edgware Road opened on 15 June.

Central London Railway

1908 Shepherd's Bush to Wood Lane opened on 14 May.

Charing Cross, Euston & Hampstead Railway

1907 Opening of line, Strand to Golders Green and Highgate (now Archway), on 22 June.

City & South London Railway

1901 Moorgate Street to Angel opened on 17 November.

1907 Angel to Euston opened on 12 May.

Great Northern, Piccadilly & Brompton Railway

1906 Opening of line, Hammersmith to Finsbury Park, on 15 December.

1907 Holborn to Strand branch opened on 30 November.

Great Northern & City Railway

1904 Opening of line on 14 February.

Metropolitan District Railway

1902 Whitechapel & Bow Railway opened, extending District services eastward, on 2 June.

1903 First electric trains from Ealing to Park Royal from 23 June and to South Harrow from 28 June.

1905 Electric trains replaced steam, Ealing Broadway to Whitechapel, from 1 June.

1905 Electric trains replaced steam, Hounslow to South Acton, from 13 June.

1905 Electric trains replaced steam, Putney Bridge to High Street Kensington, from 23 June.

1905 Electric trains replaced steam over LSWR lines, between Richmond and Turnham Green, from 18 July.

1905 Electric traction inaugurated between Whitechapel and East Ham, partly over LTSR, from 20 August.

1905 Electric trains commenced running over LSWR line between Putney Bridge and Wimbledon from 27 August.

1908 Electric traction inaugurated, East Ham to Barking over LTSR, from 1 April.

Metropolitan Railway

1904 Harrow to Uxbridge opened on 4 July.

1905 Steam replaced by electric service, Baker Street to Uxbridge, from 1 January.

1905 First stage of Inner Circle (Metropolitan and District) electrification brought into use on 1 July.

1906 Harrow-on-the-Hill to Verney Junction line via Aylesbury, and Chesham branch, leased to Metropolitan & Great Central Joint Committee for the use of Metropolitan Railway and Great Central Railway services from 2 April.

Waterloo & City Railway

1907 Absorbed by LSWR on 1 January.

PRINCIPAL AMALGAMATIONS

1902 Formation of the Underground Electric Railways Company of London Ltd, by Mr C. T. Yerkes, on 9 April.

1908 Tube railways and Metropolitan and District agree on common publicity use of the word UNDERGROUND.

1910 The Bakerloo, Hampstead and Piccadilly tubes amalgamate into the London Electric Railway as a subsidiary of the Underground Electric Railways on 1 July.

Opening dates of stations, name changes and closures

Stations opened or first served by Underground trains

1.02.1901	*West Ham [LTSR]*
17.11.1901	Angel C&SLR
17.11.1901	City Road C&SLR
17.11.1901	Old Street C&SLR
2.06.1902	Barking [LTSR] MDR
2.06.1902	Bromley [LTSR] MDR *now Bromley-By-Bow*
2.06.1902	Dagenham [LTSR] MDR *now Dagenham East*
2.06.1902	East Ham [LTSR] MDR
2.06.1902	Hornchurch [LTSR] MDR
2.06.1902	Mile End MDR
2.06.1902	Plaistow [LTSR] MDR
2.06.1902	Upton Park [LTSR] MDR
2.06.1902	Upminster [LTSR] MDR
2.06.1902	West Ham [LTSR] MDR
11.06.1902	Bow Road MDR
23.06.1902	Stepney Green MDR
1.03.1903	Hounslow Town MDR *re-opened*
1.05.1903	*Barkingside [GER]*
1.05.1903	*Chigwell [GER]*
1.05.1903	*Fairlop [GER]*
1.05.1903	*Grange Hill [GER]*
1.05.1903	*Hainault [GER]*
1.05.1903	*Newbury Park[GER]*
23.06.1903	North Ealing MDR
23.06.1903	Park Royal & Twyford Abbey MDR
28.06.1903	Perivale-Alperton MDR *now Alperton*
28.06.1903	South Harrow MDR *first site*
28.06.1903	Sudbury Hill MDR
28.06.1903	Sudbury Town MDR
14.02.1904	Drayton Park GN&CR
14.02.1904	Essex Road GN&CR
14.02.1904	Finsbury Park GN&CR
14.02.1904	Moorgate GN&CR
14.02.1904	Old Street GN&CR
1.05.1904	*Perivale GW&GC Jt*
28.06.1904	Highbury GN&CR
4.07.1904	Uxbridge MetR *first site*
4.07.1904	Ruislip MetR
1.10.1904	*Greenford GW&GC Jt*
13.06.1905	South Acton MDR
25.09.1905	Ickenham Halte MetR
9.10.1905	Barons Court MDR
10.03.1906	Baker Street BS&WR
10.03.1906	Embankment BS&WR
10.03.1906	Kennington Road BS&WR *now Lambeth North*
10.03.1906	Oxford Circus BS&WR
10.03.1906	Piccadilly Circus BS&WR
10.03.1906	Regent's Park BS&WR
10.03.1906	Trafalgar Square BS&WR *now Charing Cross*
10.03.1906	Waterloo BS&WR
2.04.1906	*Ruislip & Ickenham GW&GC Jt now West Ruislip*
26.05.1906	Eastcote Halt MetR
26.05.1906	Rayners Lane MetR
5.08.1906	Elephant & Castle BS&WR
15.12.1906	Barons Court GNP&BR
15.12.1906	Brompton Road GNP&BR
15.12.1906	Caledonian Road GNP&BR
15.12.1906	Dover Street (St.James's) GNP&BR *now Green Park*
15.12.1906	Earl's Court GNP&BR
15.12.1906	Finsbury Park GNP&BR
15.12.1906	Gillespie Road GNP&BR *now Arsenal*
15.12.1906	Gloucester Road GNP&BR
15.12.1906	Hammersmith GNP&BR
15.12.1906	Holborn GNP&BR
15.12.1906	Holloway Road GNP&BR
15.12.1906	Hyde Park Corner GNP&BR
15.12.1906	King's Cross GNP&BR
15.12.1906	Knightsbridge GNP&BR
15.12.1906	Leicester Square GNP&BR
15.12.1906	Piccadilly Circus GNP&BR
15.12.1906	Russell Square GNP&BR
15.12.1906	York Road GNP&BR
8.01.1907	South Kensington GNP&BR
15.03.1907	Down Street (Mayfair) GNP&BR
27.03.1907	Great Central BS&WR *now Marylebone*
11.04.1907	Covent Garden GNP&BR
1.05.1907	*Northolt GW&GC Jt*
12.05.1907	Euston C&SLR
12.05.1907	King's Cross for St.Pancras C&SLR
15.06.1907	Edgware Road BS&WR
22.06.1907	Belsize Park CCE&HR
22.06.1907	Camden Town CCE&HR
22.06.1907	Chalk Farm CCE&HR
22.06.1907	Charing Cross CCE&HR
22.06.1907	Euston CCE&HR
22.06.1907	Euston Road CCE&HR *now Warren Street*
22.06.1907	Golders Green CCE&HR
22.06.1907	Hampstead CCE&HR
22.06.1907	Highgate CCE&HR *now Archway*
22.06.1907	Leicester Square CCE&HR
22.06.1907	Kentish Town CCE&HR
22.06.1907	Mornington Crescent CCE&HR
22.06.1907	Oxford Street CCE&HR *now Tottenham Court*
22.06.1907	South Kentish Town CCE&HR
22.06.1907	Tottenham Court Road CCE&HR *now Goodge St.*
22.06.1907	Tufnell Park CCE&HR
30.11.1907	Strand GNP&BR *later Aldwych*
16.04.1908	Northfield (Ealing) MDR *first site*
1.05.1908	Wood Lane (Exhibition) H&CR
1.05.1908	*Northolt Junction GW&GC Jt now South Ruislip*
14.05.1908	Wood Lane CLR
21.05.1908	Preston Road MetR
2.05.1909	Hounslow Town MDR *now Hounslow East*
1.10.1909	Dollis Hill MetR
9.05.1910	Sandy Lodge MetR *now Moor Park*

Station names changed

Date	from	to
13.11.1901	Whitechapel (Mile End)	Whitechapel
1.09.1902	Putney Bridge & Fulham	Putney Bridge & Hurlingham
5.08.1906	Kennington Road	Westminster Bridge Road
1907	Westminster Bridge	Westminster
1907	Brompton (Gloucester Road)	Gloucester Road
9.03.1908	Oxford Street	Tottenham Court Road
9.03.1908	Tottenham Court Road	Goodge Street
7.06.1908	Euston Road	Warren Street
1.11.1909	Gower Street	Euston Square
1.11.1909	Bishopsgate	Liverpool Street
1.01.1910	Kingsbury & Neasden	Neasden & Kingsbury
1.03.1910	Chiswick Park & Acton Green	Chiswick Park
1.03.1910	Ealing Common & West Acton	Ealing Common
1.03.1910	Mill Hill Park	Acton Town
7.10.1910	Perivale-Alperton	Alperton
1.11.1910	Aldersgate Street	Aldersgate

Stations last served by Underground trains

31.07.1905	New Cross [LBSC] MDR
30.09.1905	Barking [LT&SR] MDR
30.09.1905	Dagenham [LT&SR] MDR
30.09.1905	Hornchurch [LT&SR] MDR
30.09.1905	Upminster [LT&SR] MDR
2.12.1906	Deptford Road [ELR] SER MetR
2.12.1906	New Cross [ELR] MetR
2.12.1906	Rotherhithe [ELR] SER MetR
2.12.1906	Shadwell & St.George-in-the-East [ELR] MetR
2.12.1906	Wapping [ELR] MetR
31.12.1906	Hammersmith (Grove Road) [LSWR] MetR *closed 1916*
1.05.1909	Hounslow Town MDR *branch terminal*

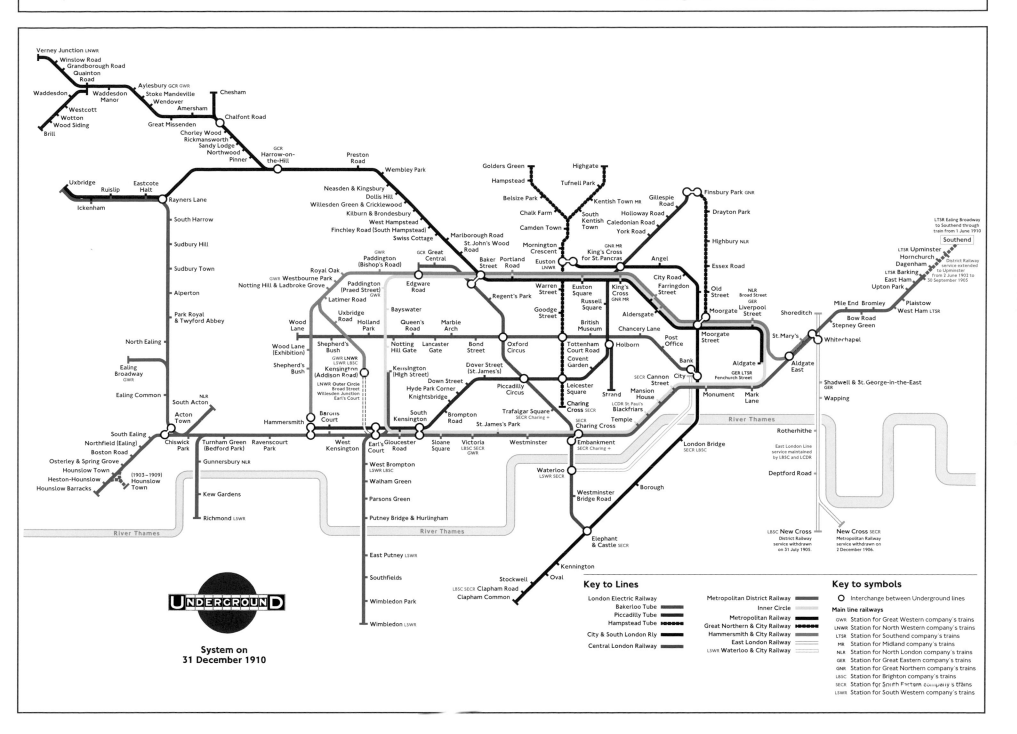

Verney Junction LNWR
Winslow Road
Grandborough Road
Quainton Road
Waddesdon
Waddesdon Manor
Aylesbury GCR GWR
Stoke Mandeville
Wendover
Westcott
Amersham
Wotton
Great Missenden
Wood Siding
Chesham
Chalfont Road
Brill
Chorley Wood
Rickmansworth
Sandy Lodge
Northwood
Pinner
GCR Harrow-on-the-Hill
Preston Road
Wembley Park

Uxbridge
Ruislip
Eastcote Halt
Ickenham
Rayners Lane
South Harrow
Sudbury Hill
Sudbury Town
Alperton
Park Royal & Twyford Abbey
North Ealing
Ealing Broadway GWR
Ealing Common
NLR South Acton
Acton Town

South Ealing
Northfield (Ealing)
Boston Road
Osterley & Spring Grove
Hounslow Town
Heston-Hounslow
Hounslow Barracks
(1903–1909) Hounslow Town
Chiswick Park
Turnham Green (Bedford Park)
Ravenscourt Park
Gunnersbury NLR
Kew Gardens
Richmond LSWR
Hammersmith

Neasden & Kingsbury
Dollis Hill
Willesden Green & Cricklewood
Kilburn & Brondesbury
West Hampstead
Finchley Road (South Hampstead)
Swiss Cottage
Marlborough Road
St. John's Wood Road

GWR Paddington (Bishop's Road)
GCR Great Central
Royal Oak
GWR Westbourne Park
Notting Hill & Ladbroke Grove
Paddington (Praed Street) GWR
Latimer Road
Uxbridge Road
Holland Park
Wood Lane
Shepherd's Bush
Wood Lane (Exhibition)
Shepherd's Bush
GWR LNWR LSWR LBSC Kensington (Addison Road)
LNWR Outer Circle Broad Street Willesden Junction Earl's Court
Barons Court
West Kensington
Earl's Court

Edgware Road
Bayswater
Queen's Road
Notting Hill Gate
Kensington (High Street)
Gloucester Road

Baker Street
Portland Road
Regent's Park
Marble Arch
Lancaster Gate
Bond Street
Down Street
Hyde Park Corner
Knightsbridge
South Kensington
Brompton Road
St. James's Park
Sloane Square
Victoria LBSC SECR GWR
Westminster

Golders Green
Hampstead
Belsize Park
Chalk Farm
Camden Town
Highgate
Tufnell Park
Kentish Town MR
South Kentish Town
Holloway Road
Caledonian Road
York Road
Mornington Crescent
Euston LNWR
Warren Street
Goodge Street
Oxford Circus
Tottenham Court Road
Covent Garden
Leicester Square
Piccadilly Circus
Dover Street (St. James's)
Trafalgar Square SECR Charing +
Charing Cross SECR

GNR MR King's Cross for St. Pancras
Euston Square
Russell Square
British Museum
King's Cross GNR MR
Chancery Lane
Holborn
Post Office
Bank
Strand
Mansion House
Temple
SECR Charing Cross

Gillespie Road
Finsbury Park GNR
Drayton Park
Highbury NLR
Essex Road
Angel
City Road
Old Street
Farringdon Street
Aldersgate
Moorgate
Moorgate Street
NLR Broad Street GER Liverpool Street
SECR Cannon Street
City
Aldgate
GER LTSR Fenchurch Street
Monument
Mark Lane
Aldgate East
Shoreditch
St. Mary's
Whitechapel

Mile End
Bromley
Bow Road
Stepney Green
West Ham LTSR
Plaistow
Shadwell & St. George-in-the-East GER
Wapping
Rotherhithe
River Thames
East London Line service maintained by LBSC and LCDR
Deptford Road

LTSR Ealing Broadway to Southend through train from 1 June 1910
Southend
LTSR Upminster
Hornchurch
Dagenham
LTSR Barking
East Ham
Upton Park
District Railway service extended to Upminster from 2 June 1902 to 30 September 1905.

LCDR St. Paul's Blackfriars
London Bridge SECR LBSC
Waterloo LSWR SECR
Westminster Bridge Road
Borough
Elephant & Castle SECR
Kennington
Stockwell
Oval
LBSC SECR Clapham Road
Clapham Common

West Brompton LSWR LBSC
Walham Green
Parsons Green
Putney Bridge & Hurlingham
East Putney LSWR
Southfields
Wimbledon Park
Wimbledon LSWR

LBSC New Cross
District Railway service withdrawn on 31 July 1905.
New Cross SECR
Metropolitan Railway service withdrawn on 2 December 1906.

UNDERGROUND

System on 31 December 1910

Key to Lines
London Electric Railway
Bakerloo Tube
Piccadilly Tube
Hampstead Tube
City & South London Rly
Central London Railway
Metropolitan District Railway
Inner Circle
Metropolitan Railway
Great Northern & City Railway
Hammersmith & City Railway
East London Railway
LSWR Waterloo & City Railway

Key to symbols
○ Interchange between Underground lines

Main line railways
GWR Station for Great Western company's trains
LNWR Station for North Western company's trains
LTSR Station for Southend company's trains
MR Station for Midland company's trains
NLR Station for North London company's trains
GER Station for Great Eastern company's trains
GNR Station for Great Northern company's trains
LBSC Station for Brighton company's trains
SECR Station for South Eastern company's trains
LSWR Station for South Western company's trains

Principal developments of the decade

Bakerloo Line

1913 Extension from Edgware Road to Paddington opened on 1 December.

1915 Extension from Paddington to Kilburn Park on 31 January and to Queen's Park on 11 February. Through running over London & North Western Railway tracks from Queen's Park to Willesden Junction commenced 10 May.

1917 Service extended over LNWR tracks from Willesden Junction to Watford Junction from 16 April.

Central London Railway

1912 Bank to Liverpool Street opened on 28 July.

1920 Inauguration of through running to Ealing Broadway over the GWR-built Ealing & Shepherd's Bush Railway on 3 August.

East London Railway

1913 Inauguration of electric trains, Shoreditch to New Cross LBSCR and New Cross SECR, on 31 March.

Great Northern & City Railway

1913 Absorbed by Metropolitan Railway on 1 June.

Metropolitan District Railway

1910 Electric train service extended from South Harrow to Rayners Lane, sharing Metropolitan Railway tracks onwards to Uxbridge, from 1 March.

1911 Through services to Southend extended to Shoeburyness.

PASS DOWN
THE PLATFORM

There are four, five, or six cars to a train. There are two gates to a car, and sometimes three. Two passengers cannot get through the same gate at the same time, but they can get through different gates at the same time. Even loading means quicker loading and in comfort.

UNDERGROUND

ELECTRIC RAILWAY HOUSE,
BROADWAY, WESTMINSTER, S.W.1

Opening dates of stations, name changes and closures

Stations opened or first served by Underground trains

1.02.1912	Stamford Brook	MDR
28.07.1912	Liverpool Street	CLR
5.08.1912	Ruislip Manor	MetR
31.03.1913	New Cross LBSC [ELR]	MetR re-opened
31.03.1913	New Cross SECR [ELR]	MetR re-opened
31.03.1913	Rotherhithe [ELR]	MetR re-opened
31.03.1913	Shadwell & St.George-in-the-East [ELR]	MetR
31.03.1913	Shoreditch [ELR]	MetR re-opened
31.03.1913	Surrey Docks [ELR]	MetR re-opened (now Surrey Quays)
31.03.1913	Wapping [ELR]	MetR re-opened
31.03.1913	Whitechapel [ELR]	re-opened
17.11.1913	West Harrow	MetR
1.12.1913	Paddington	BS&WR
1.04.1914	Goldhawk Road	MetR
1.04.1914	Shepherd's Bush	H&CR present site
6.04.1914	Charing Cross (Embankment)	CCE&HR
31.01.1915	Warwick Avenue	BS&WR
31.01.1915	Kilburn Park	BS&WR
11.02.1915	Queen's Park [LNWR]	BS&WR
22.03.1915	North Harrow	MetR
10.05.1915	Willesden Junction [LNWR]	BS&WR
6.06.1915	Maida Vale	BS&WR
1.10.1916	Kensal Green [LNWR]	BS&WR
16.04.1917	Bushey & Oxhey [LNWR]	BS&WR (now Bushey)
16.04.1917	Kenton [LNWR]	BS&WR
16.04.1917	Harlesden [LNWR]	BS&WR
16.04.1917	Harrow & Wealdstone [LNWR]	BS&WR
16.04.1917	Headstone Lane [LNWR]	BS&WR
16.04.1917	North Wembley [LNWR]	BS&WR
16.04.1917	Pinner & Hatch End [LNWR]	BS&WR (now Hatch End)
16.04.1917	Watford High Street [LNWR]	BS&WR
16.04.1917	Watford Junction [LNWR]	BS&WR
16.04.1917	Wembley for Sudbury [LNWR]	BS&WR (now Wembley Central)
1.08.1917	Stonebridge Park [LNWR]	BS&WR
1.04.1919	Ruislip Manor	MetR re-opened
5.05.1919	Carpenders Park [LNWR]	BS&WR first site
3.08.1920	Ealing Broadway [GWR]	CLR
3.08.1920	East Acton [GWR]	CLR
5.05.1920	Wood Lane (White City)	H&CR

Station names changed

	from	to
17.07.1911	Deptford Road	Surrey Docks
11.12.1911	Northfield (Ealing)	Northfields & Little Ealing
11.12.1911	Boston Road	Boston Manor
6.04.1914	Embankment [BS&WR]	Charing Cross (Embankment)
6.04.1914	Charing Cross [CCE&HR]	Charing Cross (Strand)
9.05.1915	Charing Cross (Embankment)	Charing Cross [BS&WR and CCE&HR]
9.05.1915	Charing Cross (Strand)	Strand [CCE&HR]
9.05.1915	Strand [GNP&BR]	Aldwych
1.11.1915	Chalfont Road	Chalfont & Latimer
1.11.1915	Chorley Wood	Chorley Wood & Chenies
1.03.1917	Portland Road	Great Portland Street
15.04.1917	Great Central	Marylebone
15.04.1917	Westminster Bridge Road	Lambeth (North)
1918	Shadwell & St.George-in-the-East	Shadwell re-opened
1.06.1919	Notting Hill & Ladbroke Grove	Ladbroke Grove (North Kensington)
1.02.1920	Pinner & Hatch End	Hatch End (for Pinner)
3.05.1920	Wood Lane (Exhibition)	Wood Lane (White City)
6.10.1920	Grandborough Road	Granborough Road

Stations last served by Underground trains

31.03.1914	Shepherd's Bush	MetR first site
31.10.1914	Wood Lane (Exhibition)	

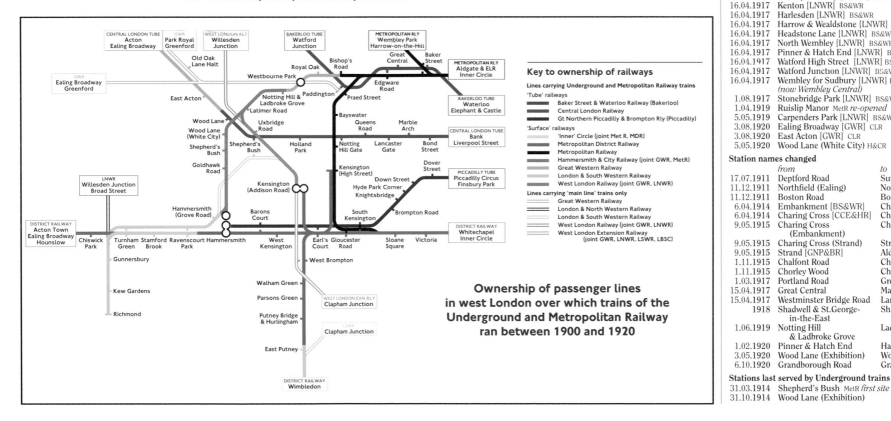

Key to ownership of railways

Lines carrying Underground and Metropolitan Railway trains

'Tube' railways
- Baker Street & Waterloo Railway (Bakerloo)
- Central London Railway
- Gt Northern Piccadilly & Brompton Rly (Piccadilly)

'Surface' railways
- 'Inner' Circle (joint Met R, MDR)
- Metropolitan District Railway
- Metropolitan Railway
- Hammersmith & City Railway (joint GWR, MetR)
- Great Western Railway
- London & South Western Railway
- West London Railway (joint GWR, LNWR)

Lines carrying 'main line' trains only
- Great Western Railway
- London & North Western Railway
- London & South Western Railway
- West London Railway (joint GWR, LNWR)
- West London Extension Railway (joint GWR, LNWR, LSWR, LBSC)

Ownership of passenger lines in west London over which trains of the Underground and Metropolitan Railway ran between 1900 and 1920

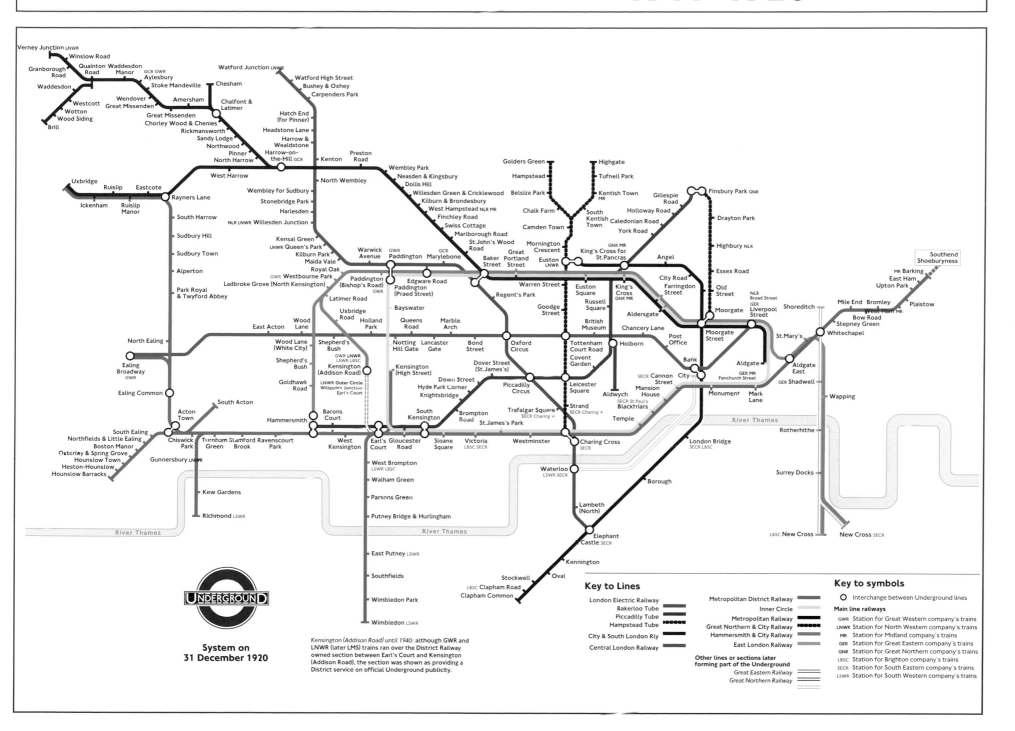

Verney Junction LNWR
Winslow Road
Granborough Road
Quainton Waddesdon Manor
Waddesdon
Aylesbury GCR GWR
Stoke Mandeville
Westcott
Wotton
Wood Siding
Brill
Wendover
Great Missenden
Amersham
Chalfont & Latimer
Chesham
Watford Junction LNWR
Watford High Street
Bushey & Oxhey
Carpenders Park
Great Missenden
Chorley Wood & Chenies
Rickmansworth
Sandy Lodge
Northwood
Pinner
North Harrow
Harrow-on-the-Hill GCR
Hatch End (for Pinner)
Headstone Lane
Harrow & Wealdstone
Kenton
Preston Road
West Harrow
North Wembley
Wembley Park
Neasden & Kingsbury
Dollis Hill
Willesden Green & Cricklewood
Kilburn & Brondesbury
West Hampstead NLR MR
Finchley Road
Swiss Cottage
Marlborough Road
St.John's Wood Road
Golders Green
Hampstead
Belsize Park
Highgate
Tufnell Park
Kentish Town MR
South Kentish Town
Chalk Farm
Camden Town
Gillespie Road
Holloway Road
Caledonian Road
York Road
Finsbury Park GNR
Drayton Park
Highbury NLR
Southend
Shoeburyness
Uxbridge
Ruislip
Eastcote
Ickenham
Ruislip Manor
Rayners Lane
Wembley for Sudbury
Stonebridge Park
Harlesden
NLR LNWR Willesden Junction
South Harrow
Sudbury Hill
Sudbury Town
Alperton
Park Royal & Twyford Abbey
Kensal Green
LNWR Queen's Park
Kilburn Park
Maida Vale
Royal Oak
GWR Westbourne Park
Ladbroke Grove (North Kensington)
Warwick Avenue
GWR Paddington
GCR Marylebone
Baker Street
Great Portland Street
Euston LNWR
Mornington Crescent
King's Cross for St.Pancras GNR MR
Angel
Essex Road
MR Barking
East Ham
Upton Park
Mile End MR
West Ham MR
Bow Road
Stepney Green
Plaistow
North Ealing
Ealing Broadway GWR
Ealing Common
East Acton
Wood Lane
Paddington (Bishop's Road)
Uxbridge Road
Holland Park
Latimer Road
Paddington (Praed Street) GWR
Edgware Road
Bayswater
Queens Road
Marble Arch
Regent's Park
Warren Street
Goodge Street
Euston Square
King's Cross GNR MR
Russell Square
City Road
Farringdon Street
Old Street
Moorgate
NLR Broad Street
GER Liverpool Street
Shoreditch
Whitechapel
Acton Town
South Acton
Goldhawk Road
Shepherd's Bush
GWR LNWR LSWR LBSC
Kensington (Addison Road)
LNWR Outer Circle Willesden Junction Earl's Court
Shepherd's Bush
Wood Lane (White City)
Notting Hill Gate
Lancaster Gate
Bond Street
Oxford Circus
Tottenham Court Road
Holborn
Chancery Lane
Post Office
Bank
Aldersgate
British Museum
Moorgate Street
Aldgate
St.Mary's
Aldgate East
GER MR Fenchurch Street
GER Shadwell
Wapping
Kensington (High Street)
Down Street
Hyde Park Corner
Knightsbridge
Dover Street (St.James's)
Piccadilly Circus
Leicester Square
Covent Garden
Aldwych
SECR Cannon Street
Mansion House
SECR St.Paul's Blackfriars
City
Monument
Mark Lane
Hammersmith
Barons Court
West Kensington
Earl's Court
Gloucester Road
South Kensington
Sloane Square
Brompton Road
St.James's Park
Trafalgar Square SECR Charing +
Strand SECR Charing +
Temple
Westminster
Charing Cross SECR
London Bridge SECR LBSC
River Thames
Rotherhithe
Chiswick Park
Turnham Green
Stamford Brook
Ravenscourt Park
Victoria LBSC SECR
South Ealing
Northfields & Little Ealing
Boston Manor
Osterley & Spring Grove
Hounslow Town
Heston-Hounslow
Hounslow Barracks
Gunnersbury LNWR
West Brompton LSWR LBSC
Walham Green
Parsons Green
Putney Bridge & Hurlingham
Waterloo LSWR SECR
Lambeth (North)
Borough
Surrey Docks
Kew Gardens
Richmond LSWR
East Putney LSWR
Southfields
Wimbledon Park
Wimbledon LSWR
Elephant & Castle SECR
Kennington
LBSC New Cross
New Cross SECR
Stockwell
LBSC Clapham Road
Clapham Common
Oval

Kensington (Addison Road) until 1940: although GWR and LNWR (later LMS) trains ran over the District Railway owned section between Earl's Court and Kensington (Addison Road), the section was shown as providing a District service on official Underground publicity.

Key to Lines

London Electric Railway
  Bakerloo Tube
  Piccadilly Tube
  Hampstead Tube
City & South London Rly
Central London Railway

Metropolitan District Railway
  Inner Circle
Metropolitan Railway
Great Northern & City Railway
Hammersmith & City Railway
East London Railway

**Other lines or sections later
forming part of the Underground**
  Great Eastern Railway
  Great Northern Railway

Key to symbols

◯ Interchange between Underground lines

Main line railways

GWR Station for Great Western company's trains
LNWR Station for North Western company's trains
MR Station for Midland company's trains
GER Station for Great Eastern company's trains
GNR Station for Great Northern company's trains
LBSC Station for Brighton company's trains
SECR Station for South Eastern company's trains
LSWR Station for South Western company's trains

Principal developments of the decade

Centre right The entrance to Hendon Central station as first built in open countryside in November 1923.

Far right The same station entrance once it had been enveloped by shops and flats at the end of the same decade.

Right The original Piccadilly Circus booking hall connected to the platforms by lifts was replaced, from 1928, by the present circular concourse and eleven escalators. Many of the original features can still be seen, such as the world clock and panelled ceiling. Others, sadly missing, are the fluted ceiling lampshades either side of the columns which were destroyed when fluorescent lighting was installed in the 1950s, but not re-instated when the concourse was restored.

Below Detail from a poster of the 1920s showing a typical tube station, with a train of Standard Stock.

Hampstead & Highgate Line and City & South London Railway

1922 Euston to Moorgate closed for enlargement of tunnels, on 8 August.

1923 Golders Green to Hendon opened on 19 November.

1923 Moorgate to Clapham Common closed for enlargement of tunnels, on 28 November.

1924 Moorgate to Euston re-opened on 20 April following enlargement of tunnels, allowing through running to be inaugurated via Camden Town to join the Hampstead & Highgate Line.

1924 Hendon to Edgware opened from 18 August.

1924 Moorgate to Clapham Common re-opened with enlarged tunnels, on 1 December.

1926 Clapham Common to Morden, and through running via Kennington to Hampstead & Highgate Line, from 13 September.

Metropolitan Railway

1925 Branch from north of Moor Park & Sandy Lodge to Watford, with one intermediate station at Croxley Green, opened with a joint service with the LNER on 2 November.

Piccadilly Line

1930 Civil engineering commenced on extensions to both ends, from Finsbury Park towards Arnos Grove in the north and from Hammersmith towards Acton Town in the west.

Opening dates of stations, name changes and closures

Stations opened or first served by Underground trains

28.06.1923	Northwick Park & Kenton	MetR
5.11.1923	North Acton	CLR [GWR]
5.11.1923	West Acton	CLR [GWR]
19.11.1923	Brent	CCE&HR *(now Brent Cross)*
19.11.1923	Hendon Central	CCE&HR
10.12.1923	Hillingdon	Met MDR
18.08.1924	Colindale	CCE&HR
18.08.1924	Edgware	CCE&HR
27.10.1924	Burnt Oak	CCE&HR
2.11.1925	Croxley Green	MetR-LNER JOINT *(now Croxley)*
2.11.1925	Watford	MetR-LNER JOINT
28.06.1926	Gale Street	LMS *(now Becontree)*
13.09.1926	Clapham South	C&SLR
13.09.1926	Colliers Wood	C&SLR
13.09.1926	Morden	C&SLR
13.09.1926	South Wimbledon	C&SLR
13.09.1926	Tooting Broadway	C&SLR
13.09.1926	Trinity Road (Tooting Bec)	C&SLR
13.09.1926	Waterloo	CCE&HR
6.12.1926	Balham	C&SLR

Station names changed

	from	*to*
26.01.1922	Farringdon Street	Farringdon & High Holborn
12.03.1922	Amersham	Amersham & Chesham Bois
20.07.1922	Essex Road	Canonbury & Essex Road
20.07.1922	Highbury	Highbury & Islington
20.07.1922	Bayswater	Bayswater (Queen's Road) & Westbourne Grove
1.10.1922	Waddesdon Manor	Waddesdon
1.10.1922	Waddesdon [O&AT]	Waddesdon Road
1923	Great Portland Street	Great Portland Street & Regent's Park
1923	Aldersgate	Aldersgate & Barbican
26.01.1923	St.Mary's	St.Mary's (Whitechapel Road)
9.07.1923	New Cross [LBSC]	New Cross Gate
18.10.1923	Sandy Lodge	Moor Park & Sandy Lodge
11.02.1924	West Ham	West Ham (Manor Road)
20.04.1924	Moorgate Street [C&SLR]	Moorgate
1925	King's Cross [MetR]	King's Cross & St.Pancras
1.04.1925	St.John's Wood Road	St.John's Wood
1.12.1925	Hounslow Town	Hounslow East
1.12.1925	Heston - Hounslow	Hounslow Central
1.12.1925	Hounslow Barracks	Hounslow West
13.09.1926	Clapham Road	Clapham North
1927	King's Cross [GNP&BR]	King's Cross for St.Pancras
c.1928	Burnt Oak	Burnt Oak (Watling)
c.1928	Lambeth (North)	Lambeth North
c.1928	South Wimbledon	South Wimbledon (Merton)
1.03.1928	Mill Hill [LNER]	Mill Hill (East) for Mill Hill Burracks [LNER]
1929	Snaresbrook & Wanstead	Snaresbrook for Wanstead

Stations last served by Underground trains

8.08.1922	City Road	C&SLR
5.06.1924	South Kentish Town	CCE&HR

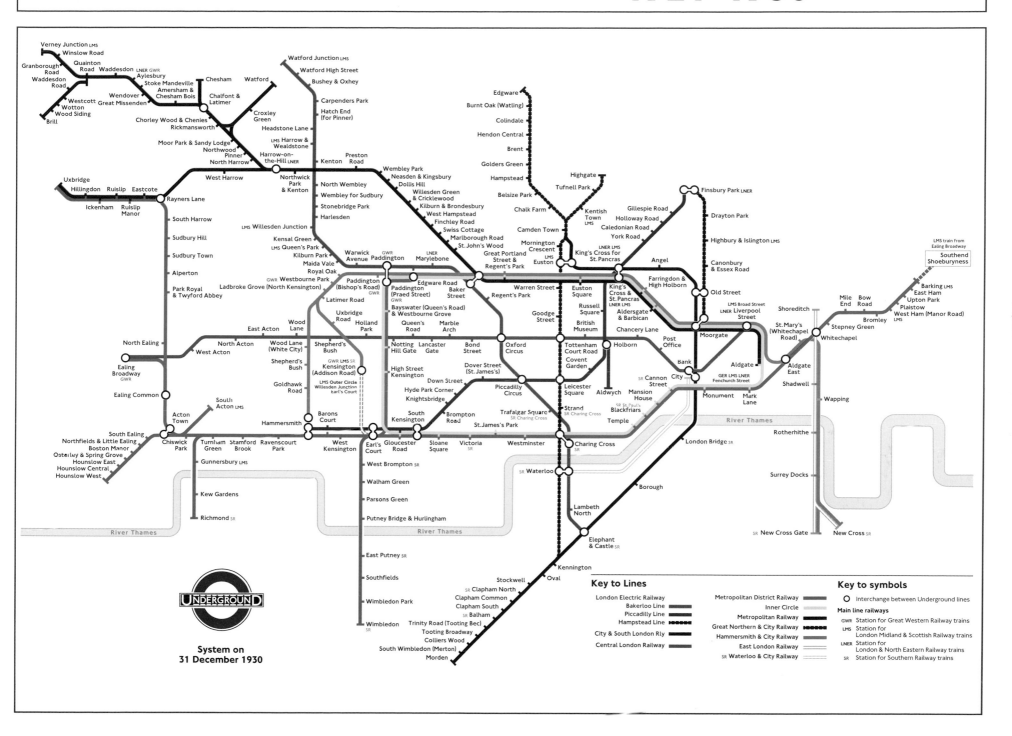

**System on
31 December 1930**

Key to Lines

London Electric Railway		Metropolitan District Railway	
Bakerloo Line		Inner Circle	
Piccadilly Line		Metropolitan Railway	
Hampstead Line		Great Northern & City Railway	
City & South London Rly		Hammersmith & City Railway	
Central London Railway		East London Railway	
		SR Waterloo & City Railway	

Key to symbols

○ Interchange between Underground lines

Main line railways

GWR Station for Great Western Railway trains
LMS Station for London Midland & Scottish Railway trains
LNER Station for London & North Eastern Railway trains
SR Station for Southern Railway trains

Principal developments of the decade

Above right One era closes as another opens. The Metropolitan Line's tranquil Granborough Road station, which lost its passenger service in 1936, contrasts with a 'streamlined' tube train of 1935.

Below Osterley station, new in 1934, was one of a number designed in the 1920s and '30s for the Underground by the architect Charles Holden.

Bakerloo Line

1939 Bakerloo trains run to Stanmore, through new tunnels from Baker Street to Finchley Road and over former Metropolitan tracks, from 20 November.

Central London Railway

1933 Became Central London Line of LPTB on 1 July.

1937 Was re-named the Central Line from 28 August.

C&SLR and Hampstead & Highgate Line

1933 Both combined as the Edgware, Highgate & Morden Line of the London Passenger Transport Board on 1 July.

1934 Re-named Morden–Edgware Line.

1937 In preparation for the opening of the extensions to Edgware (via Mill Hill), High Barnet and Alexandra Palace the line was renamed Northern Line, from 28 August.

1939 Electric traction to East Finchley from 3 July.

1940 Electric traction to High Barnet from 14 April.

Great Northern & City Railway

1933 Became the Great Northern & City Line on 1 July, and then Northern City Line October 1934.

1939 Original main line size rolling stock replaced by Tube stock on 15 May, in preparation for the line's amalgamation with the Northern Line.

Hammersmith & City Line

1936 First Class abolished on H&C trains from 4 May.

1940 Service suspended between Latimer Road and Kensington (Addison Road) on 19 October.

Metropolitan Railway

1932 Branch to Stanmore opened on 10 December.

1933 Became the Metropolitan Line of the London Passenger Transport Board on 1 July.

1933 Passenger service between Rickmansworth and Watford withdrawn on 31 December.

1939 Haulage of GWR Hayes, Uxbridge and Windsor trains by Metropolitan electric locomotives discontinued between Paddington and Aldgate on 16 September.

1939 Pullman cars withdrawn from trains between Aylesbury / Chesham and Aldgate on 7 October.

1940 First Class accommodation withdrawn from Harrow and Uxbridge trains from 1 February.

Metropolitan District Railway

1932 Extended from Barking to Upminster over LMS line on 12 September.

1933 Became the District Line on 1 July.

1933 District Line service between Ealing and Uxbridge transferred to Piccadilly Line operation from 23 October.

1940 LMS-operated Outer Circle Willesden – Earl's Court service withdrawn on 2 October.

Piccadilly Line

1932 Tube trains start working over District Line to South Harrow via Hammersmith and Acton Town from 4 July.

1932 Finsbury Park to Arnos Grove from 19 September.

1933 Arnos Grove to Enfield West, with through services to Hounslow West, from 13 March.

1933 Enfield West to Cockfosters from 31 July.

1933 Through service to Uxbridge from 23 October.

1940 Aldwych branch and station closed on 21 September.

PRINCIPAL AMALGAMATIONS

1933 London Transport acquired the City & South London Railway, the Central London Railway, the London Electric Railway, the Metropolitan Railway and the Metropolitan District Railway, on 1 July.

Station names changed

	from	to
1931	Dollis Hill	Dollis Hill & Gladstone Park
1931	King's Cross & St.Pancras MetR	King's Cross St.Pancras
1932	Putney Bridge & Hurlingham	Putney Bridge
1.01.1932	Neasden & Kingsbury	Neasden
18.07.1932	Gale Street [LMS]	Becontree
12.09.1932	Northolt Junction [GWR]	South Ruislip & Northolt Junction
31.10.1932	Gillespie Road	Arsenal (Highbury Hill)
1933	Bayswater (Queen's Road) & Westbourne Grove	Bayswater (Queen's Road)
1933	Canons Park (Edgware)	Canons Park
1933	Dollis Hill & Gladstone Park	Dollis Hill
1933	Great Portland Street & Regent's Park	Great Portland Street
1933	King's Cross for St.Pancras	King's Cross St.Pancras
22.05.1933	Holborn	Holborn (Kingsway)
10.09.1933	Paddington (Bishop's Road)	Paddington
18.09.1933	Dover Street (St.James's)	Green Park
c.1934	Amersham & Chesham Bois	Amersham
1934	Chorley Wood & Chenies	Chorley Wood
20.04.1934	Hillingdon	Hillingdon (Swakeleys)
3.05.1934	Enfield West	Enfield West (Oakwood)
25.06.1934	Chancery Lane	Chancery Lane (Gray's Inn)
1.03.1936	Park Royal	Park Royal (Hanger Hill)
21.04.1936	Farringdon & High Holborn	Farringdon
1.02.1937	Post Office	St.Paul's
15.03.1937	Northwick Park & Kenton	Northwick Park
5.07.1937	George Lane [LNER]	South Woodford (George Lane) [LNER]
1938	Ladbroke Grove (North Kensington)	Ladbroke Grove
1938	Willesden Green & Cricklewood	Willesden Green
11.06.1939	Highgate	Archway (Highgate)
11.06.1939	St.John's Wood MET	Lord's
1.04.1940	Finchley (Church End)	Finchley Central [LNER]
28.10.1940	City [Waterloo & City]	Bank [Waterloo & City]

Stations last served by Underground trains

5.07.1931	Park Royal & Twyford Abbey MDR
21.11.1931	Preston Road London-bound side MetR *first site*
2.01.1932	Preston Road country-bound side MetR *first site*
18.05.1932	Northfields & Little Ealing LER - PICCADILLY *first site*
21.05.1932	Down Street LER - PICCADILLY
17.09.1932	York Road LER - PICCADILLY
24.09.1933	British Museum CENTRAL LONDON LINE
24.03.1934	Osterley & Spring Grove DISTRICT/PICCADILLY LINES *first site*
29.07.1934	Brompton Road PICCADILLY LINE
30.11.1935	Brill METROPOLITAN LINE
30.11.1935	Waddesdon Road METROPOLITAN LINE
30.11.1935	Westcott METROPOLITAN LINE
30.11.1935	Wood Siding METROPOLITAN LINE
30.11.1935	Wotton METROPOLITAN LINE
4.07.1936	Granborough Road [Met&GCJt] METROPOLITAN LINE
4.07.1936	Winslow Road [Met&GCJt] METROPOLITAN LINE
4.07.1936	Verney Junction [Met&GCJt] MET LINE *still served by LMS*
5.07.1936	Quainton Road [Met&GCJt] MET LINE *still served by LNER*
5.07.1936	Waddesdon [Met&GCJt] MET LINE *still served by LNER*
30.04.1938	St.Mary's DISTRICT/METROPOLITAN LINES
30.10.1938	Aldgate East DISTRICT/METROPOLITAN LINES *first site*
3.12.1938	Uxbridge METROPOLITAN/PICCADILLY LINES *first site*
19.11.1939	Marlborough Road METROPOLITAN LINE
19.11.1939	Lord's METROPOLITAN LINE
17.08.1940	Swiss Cottage METROPOLITAN LINE
21.09.1940	Aldwych PICCADILLY LINE *temporary closure*
19.10.1940	Kensington (Addison Road) [WLR]
19.10.1940	Uxbridge Road [WLR] METROPOLITAN LINE

Leaflets were produced at an ever increasing rate advertising the new extensions as they were opened.

Opening dates of stations, name changes and closures

Stations opened or first served by Underground trains

6.07.1931	Park Royal MDR *present site*
22.11.1931	Preston Road *London-bound side* MetR *present site*
3.01.1932	Preston Road *country-bound side* MetR *present site*
19.05.1932	Northfields MDR *present site*
12.09.1932	Becontree [LMS] MDR
12.09.1932	Dagenham [LMS] MDR *re-served (now Dagenham East)*
12.09.1932	Heathway [LMS] MDR *(now Dagenham Heathway)*
12.09.1932	Hornchurch [LMS] MDR *re-served*
12.09.1932	Upminster [LMS] MDR *re-served*
12.09.1932	Upney [LMS] MDR
19.09.1932	Arnos Grove LER - PICCADILLY
19.09.1932	Bounds Green LER - PICCADILLY
19.09.1932	Manor House LER - PICCADILLY
19.09.1932	Turnpike Lane LER - PICCADILLY
19.09.1932	Wood Green LER - PICCADILLY
10.12.1932	Canons Park (Edgware) MetR
10.12.1932	Kingsbury MetR
10.12.1932	Stanmore MetR
1.03.1933	West Finchley [LNER]
13.03.1933	Enfield West LER - PICCADILLY *now Oakwood*
13.03.1933	Southgate LER - PICCADILLY
3.07.1933	South Kenton [LMS] BAKERLOO LINE
31.07.1933	Cockfosters PICCADILLY LINE
25.09.1933	Holborn (Kingsway) CENTRAL LONDON LINE
13.11.1933	Northwood Hills METROPOLITAN LINE
25.03.1934	Osterley DISTRICT/PICCADILLY LINES *present site*
09.07.1934	Ruislip Gardens [GWR]
16.12.1934	Queensbury METROPOLITAN LINE
17.12.1934	Upminster Bridge [LMS] DISTRICT LINE
13.05.1935	Elm Park [LMS] DISTRICT LINE
3.02.1936	Roding Valley [LNER]
31.10.1938	Aldgate East DISTRICT/METROPOLITAN LINES *present site*
4.12.1938	Uxbridge METROPOLITAN/PICCADILLY LINES *present site*
3.07.1939	East Finchley [LNER] NORTHERN LINE
20.11.1939	Finchley Road BAKERLOO LINE
20.11.1939	St.John's Wood BAKERLOO LINE
20.11.1939	Swiss Cottage BAKERLOO LINE
14.04.1940	Finchley Central [LNER] NORTHERN LINE
14.04.1940	High Barnet [LNER] NORTHERN LINE
14.04.1940	Totteridge & Whetstone [LNER] NORTHERN LINE
14.04.1940	West Finchley [LNER] NORTHERN LINE
14.04.1940	Woodside Park [LNER] NORTHERN LINE

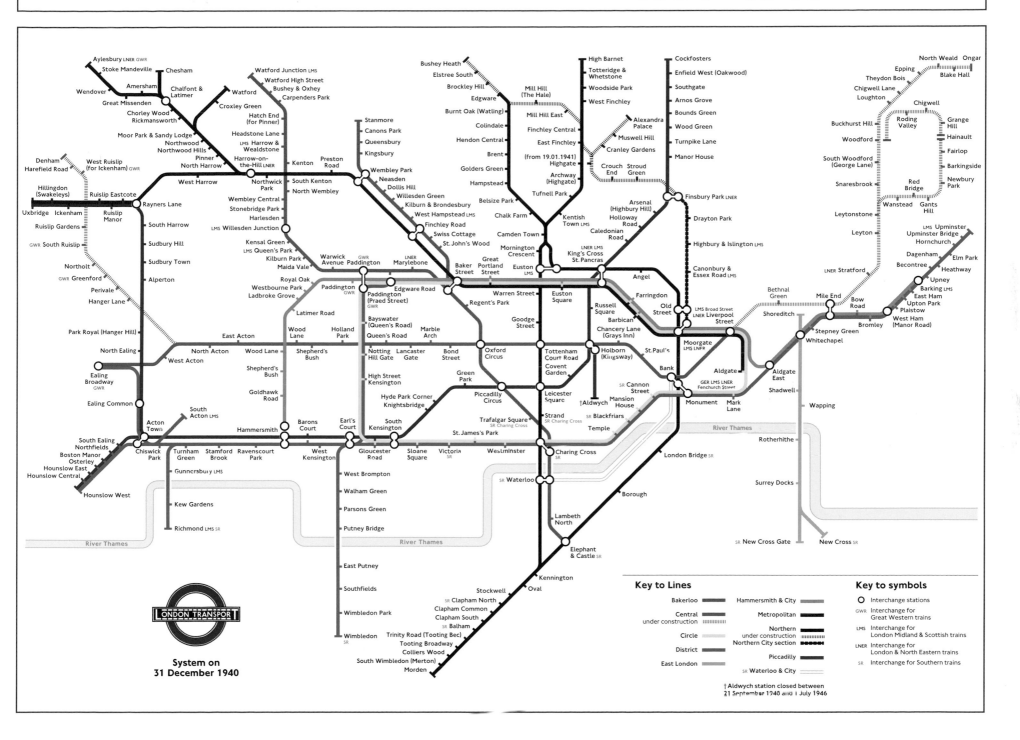

System on
31 December 1940

Key to Lines

Bakerloo	Hammersmith & City
Central	Metropolitan
under construction	Northern
Circle	under construction
	Northern City section
District	Piccadilly
East London	SR Waterloo & City

Key to symbols

○ Interchange stations

GWR Interchange for Great Western trains

LMS Interchange for London Midland & Scottish trains

LNER Interchange for London & North Eastern trains

SR Interchange for Southern trains

†Aldwych station closed between 21 September 1940 and 1 July 1946

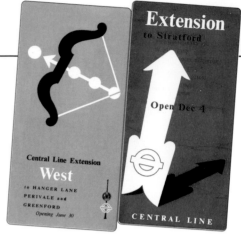

Extension
to Stratford

Open Dec 4

Central Line Extension
West
to HANGER LANE
PERIVALE and
GREENFORD
Opening June 30

CENTRAL LINE

Principal developments of the decade

Northern Line

1941 The new Highgate tube station, which also included rebuilt surface level platforms for interchange with the Alexandra Palace branch in course of conversion to Northern Line operation, opened on 19 January.

1941 Electric trains commenced running over Finchley Central to Mill Hill East branch on 18 May.

Metropolitan Line

1941 First Class withdrawn from Aylesbury and Watford trains from 6 October.

Central Line

1946 First post-war extension from Liverpool Street to Stratford opened on 4 December.

1947 Eastern extension to Leytonstone opened on 5 May.

1947 Western extension from North Acton to Greenford opened on 30 June.

1947 Both branches opened from Leytonstone: one through tube tunnels to Newbury Park; the other over LNER tracks to Woodford, on 14 December.

1948 Newbury Park to Hainault electric service replaced British Railways steam trains from 31 May.

1948 Eastern Region steam trains replaced on the extension from Woodford to Loughton and the branch from Loughton to Hainault via Roding Valley from 21 November. On same day, electric services to West Ruislip replaced local Western Region steam trains.

1949 Electric trains replaced Eastern Region steam from Loughton to Epping on 25 September.

Piccadilly Line

1946 Aldwych branch and station re-opened on 1 July.

Above Acton Town in August 1948, with a Piccadilly Line train of Standard Stock ready to leave for Hounslow, while a District Line train headed by an E Class motor car of 1914 with hand operated doors, stands at the eastbound platform.

Centre The trains introduced by the Metropolitan Railway in the 1920s and used on the Circle Line service lasted until the very end of this decade, the last of the class being withdrawn on 31 December 1950.

Above right Maps displayed in the advertisement panels of compartment stock, tracing the Metropolitan Line's country network, employed two distinct styles: that showing the steam section to Aylesbury was drawn in a geographic style reflecting the leisurely tone associated with the mode of travel, while that covering the electrified section was drawn to the prevailing diagram standards.

Opening dates of stations, name changes and closures

Stations opened or first served by Underground trains

19.01.1941	Highgate	NORTHERN LINE *present site*
14.03.1941	King's Cross St.Pancras	METROPOLITAN LINE *present site*
18.05.1941	Mill Hill East [LNER]	NORTHERN LINE
3.05.1943	Quainton Road	METROPOLITAN LINE *station re-served*
1.07.1946	Aldwych	PICCADILLY LINE
4.12.1946	Bethnal Green	CENTRAL LINE
4.12.1946	Mile End	CENTRAL LINE
4.12.1946	Stratford [LNER]	CENTRAL LINE
20.12.1946	Kensington (Olympia)	DISTRICT LINE *exhibitions only*
5.05.1947	Leyton [LNER]	CENTRAL LINE
5.05.1947	Leytonstone [LNER]	CENTRAL LINE
30.06.1947	Greenford [GWR]	CENTRAL LINE
30.06.1947	Hanger Lane [GWR]	CENTRAL LINE
30.06.1947	Perivale [GWR]	CENTRAL LINE
23.11.1947	White City	CENTRAL LINE
14.12.1947	Gants Hill	CENTRAL LINE
14.12.1947	Newbury Park [LNER]	CENTRAL LINE
14.12.1947	Redbridge	CENTRAL LINE
14.12.1947	South Woodford (George Lane) [LNER]	CENTRAL LINE
14.12.1947	Snaresbrook [LNER]	CENTRAL LINE
14.12.1947	Wanstead	CENTRAL LINE
14.12.1947	Woodford [LNER]	CENTRAL LINE

31.05.1948	Barkingside BR[E]	CENTRAL LINE
31.05.1948	Fairlop BR[E]	CENTRAL LINE
31.05.1948	Hainault BR[E]	CENTRAL LINE
21.11.1948	Buckhurst Hill	CENTRAL LINE
21.11.1948	Chigwell	CENTRAL LINE
21.11.1948	Grange Hill	CENTRAL LINE
21.11.1948	Loughton	CENTRAL LINE
21.11.1948	Northolt	CENTRAL LINE
21.11.1948	Roding Valley	CENTRAL LINE
21.11.1948	Ruislip Gardens	CENTRAL LINE
21.11.1948	South Ruislip	CENTRAL LINE
21.11.1948	West Ruislip (for Ickenham)	CENTRAL LINE
25.09.1949	Blake Hall	CENTRAL LINE *operated by BR[E]*
25.09.1949	Debden	CENTRAL LINE
25.09.1949	Epping	CENTRAL LINE
25.09.1949	North Weald	CENTRAL LINE *operated by BR[E]*
25.09.1949	Ongar	CENTRAL LINE *operated by BR[E]*
25.09.1949	Theydon Bois	CENTRAL LINE

Stations last served by Underground trains

9.03.1941	King's Cross	METROPOLITAN LINE *first site*
22.11.1947	Wood Lane	CENTRAL LINE
29.05.1948	Quainton Road	METROPOLITAN LINE *still open for BR[E]*

Station names changed

Date	from	to
18.05.1941	Mill Hill (East) for Mill Hill Barracks	Mill Hill East
1.09.1946	Bayswater (Queen's Road)	Bayswater (Queensway)
1.09.1946	Enfield West (Oakwood)	Oakwood
1.09.1946	Mark Lane	Tower Hill
1.09.1946	Queen's Road	Queensway
19.12.1946	*Kensington (Addison Road)*	*Kensington (Olympia)*
1947	Park Royal (Hanger Hill)	Park Royal
30.06.1947	South Ruislip & Northolt Junction [GWR]	South Ruislip
30.06.1947	Ruislip & Ickenham [GWR]	West Ruislip
23.11.1947	Wood Lane (White City)	White City
12.1947	Archway (Highgate)	Archway
14.12.1947	Snaresbrook for Wanstead	Snaresbrook
5.07.1948	Wembley for Sudbury	Wembley Central
11.07.1948	Canonbury & Essex Road	Essex Road
11.07.1948	Paddington (Praed Street)	Paddington
1.05.1949	Dagenham	Dagenham East
1.05.1949	Heathway	Dagenham Heathway
23.05.1949	Croxley Green	Croxley
25.09.1949	Chigwell Lane	Debden
25.09.1949	South Woodford (George Lane)	South Woodford
25.09.1950	Aylesbury [BR(E)]	Aylesbury Town [BR(E)]
25.09.1950	Moor Park & Sandy Lodge	Moor Park
25.09.1950	Kilburn & Brondesbury	Kilburn
1.10.1950	Trinity Road (Tooting Bec)	Tooting Bec

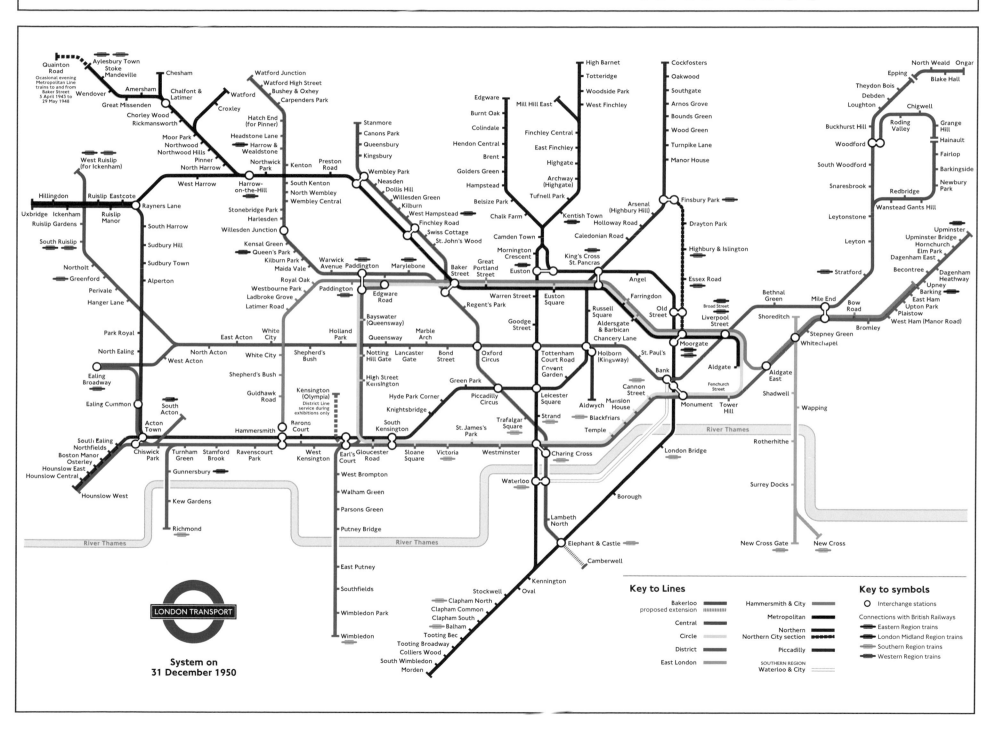

System on
31 December 1950

Key to Lines

Bakerloo	Hammersmith & City
proposed extension	Metropolitan
Central	Northern
Circle	Northern City section
District	Piccadilly
East London	SOUTHERN REGION Waterloo & City

Key to symbols

○ Interchange stations

Connections with British Railways
- Eastern Region trains
- London Midland Region trains
- Southern Region trains
- Western Region trains

Principal developments of the decade

District Line

1953 First train of unpainted aluminium stock enters service on 19 January.

Northern Line

1954 Official abandonment, on 9 February, of all unfinished portions of the pre-war new works scheme. These were: extension beyond Edgware to Bushey Heath; electrification of steam worked line beyond Mill Hill East to Edgware; connection between Finsbury Park and Highgate; Alexandra Palace branch from Highgate.

Central Line

1957 Tube stock replaced the steam trains provided by British Railways Eastern Region on the single line Epping – Ongar section, on 18 November. This completed the 82.48km (51¼ mile) programme of Central Line extensions and electrictrification of former main line routes.

Metropolitan Line

1960 The electrified rails reached out to Amersham and Chesham on 12 September 1960.

Opening dates of stations, name changes and closures

Stations opened or first served by Underground trains
17.11.1952   Carpenders Park   BAKERLOO LINE *present site*

Station names changed

	from	*to*
2.03.1952	Walham Green	Fulham Broadway
11.06.1956	Hatch End (for Pinner)	Hatch End

Stations last served by Underground trains
16.11.1952   Carpenders Park   BAKERLOO LINE *first site*
28.02.1959   South Acton   DISTRICT LINE *remained open for BR(M)*
24.10.1959   White City   METROPOLITAN LINE

One of the Underground's first unpainted aluminium cars of R Stock for the District Line, which entered service in 1953.

Epping had been the eastern terminal point of the electrified Central Line since 25 September 1949, leaving the single line extension to Ongar steam operated until 18 November 1957. A British Railways Eastern Region shuttle train waits at Epping for the Central Line tube to arrive from London, before returning to Ongar in the early 1950s.

A system of directions to central London main line terminal stations, using colour coded lights, guided passengers through interchanges between lines.

But the main problem was that the directional colours to be followed often differed from those of the lines to be used, which led to this fundamentally useful idea being abandoned.

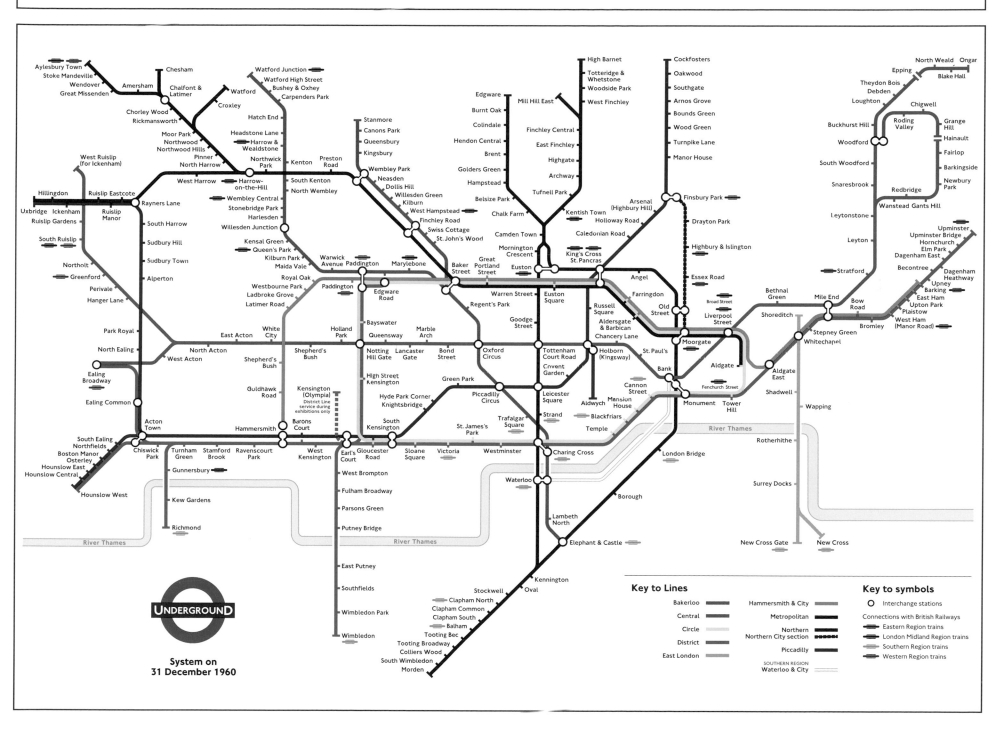

UNDERGROUND

**System on
31 December 1960**

Key to Lines

Bakerloo	Hammersmith & City
Central	Metropolitan
Circle	Northern
District	Northern City section
East London	Piccadilly

SOUTHERN REGION
Waterloo & City

Key to symbols

○ Interchange stations

Connections with British Railways

Eastern Region trains
London Midland Region trains
Southern Region trains
Western Region trains

Principal developments of the decade

Central Line

1964 The Woodford – Hainault section was experimentally converted for automatic train operation using 1960 stock trains of suitably equipped motor cars with refurbished pre-war trailer cars. Apart from some tests of equipment on the District Line, this was the first use of automatic train operation on London's Underground.

Metropolitan Line

1961 Full through electric service introduced between Baker Street and Amersham and on the Chesham branch. Withdrawal of Metropolitan Line trains north of Amersham – the manning of stations and operation of the diesel train service beyond was transferred completely to British Railways London Midland Region – after 9 September.

Northern Line – Northern City section

1964 Drayton Park becomes the northern terminus, as a consequence of the Finsbury Park station tunnels being adapted to form part of the Victoria Line, after 3 October.

Victoria Line

1962 The Government sanctions the building of the Victoria Line – between Victoria and Walthamstow (Hoe Street) – a distance of 16.1km (10½ miles).

1968 The initial section of London's first new Underground line for 60 years opened between Walthamstow Central and Highbury & Islington on 1 September. Its automatic operation and trains were evolved from the experimental prototypes developed on the Woodford – Hainault section of the Central Line.

1968 Services commenced on the second section between Highbury & Islington and Warren Street on 1 December.

1969 The line through to Victoria was opened by Queen Elizabeth II on 7 March.

Opening dates of stations, name changes and closures

Stations opened or first served by Underground trains

5.02.1967	Tower Hill	DISTRICT LINE *present site*
1.09.1968	Blackhorse Road	VICTORIA LINE
1.09.1968	Finsbury Park	VICTORIA LINE
1.09.1968	Highbury & Islington	VICTORIA LINE
1.09.1968	Seven Sisters	VICTORIA LINE
1.09.1968	Tottenham Hale	VICTORIA LINE
1.09.1968	Walthamstow Central	VICTORIA LINE
1.12.1968	Euston	VICTORIA LINE
1.12.1968	King's Cross St.Pancras	VICTORIA LINE
1.12.1968	Warren Street	VICTORIA LINE
7.03.1969	Green Park	VICTORIA LINE
7.03.1969	Oxford Circus	VICTORIA LINE
7.03.1969	Victoria	VICTORIA LINE

Station names changed

	from	*to*
1965	Chorley Wood	Chorleywood
18.05.1967	Bromley	Bromley-by-Bow
6.05.1968	*Hoe Street Walthamstow*	*Walthamstow Central*
1.12.1968	Aldersgate & Barbican	Barbican
1.01.1969	West Ham (Manor Road)	West Ham

Stations last served by Underground trains

9.09.1961	Great Missenden	METROPOLITAN LINE *transferred to BR*
9.09.1961	Wendover	METROPOLITAN LINE *transferred to BR*
9.09.1961	Stoke Mandeville	METROPOLITAN LINE *transferred to BR*
9.09.1961	Aylesbury Town [BR]	METROPOLITAN LINE *remained open for BR*
3.10.1964	Finsbury Park	NORTHERN CITY
4.02.1967	Tower Hill	DISTRICT LINE *first site*

Part of the fleet of automatic trains pose outside their Northumberland Park depot prior to the opening of the Victoria Line in 1968.

VICTORIA LINE ⊖
Exhibition at the Design Centre
August 21 – September 28, 1968
SOUVENIR TICKET

A Metropolitan Line steam train runs for the last time on the Chalfont & Latimer to Chesham branch. In 1936 haulage of LT passenger trains was devolved to LNER (and later British Railways) engines and crews. The carriages remained LT property and those used on the Chesham branch held the distinction of being the oldest in the fleet, dating from 1898.

Peggy Healey, of London Transport's Publicity Office, tries out the experimental automatic gates at Hammersmith District and Piccadilly lines ticket office.

SOUTH KENSINGTON (D) 2
To any one of L.T. stations shown on fares list at SINGLE FARE of   **1/3**
For automatic gates
INSERT THIS WAY →
Issued subject to LONDON TRANSPORT Bye-laws, Regulations and Conditions. Valid day of issue only.

LONDON TRANSPORT   1
LAST DAY OF STEAM SHUTTLE OPERATION
11th SEPTEMBER, 1960
CHALFONT & LATIMER
to
CHESHAM
2nd Cl.   Fare 10d
For conditions see over

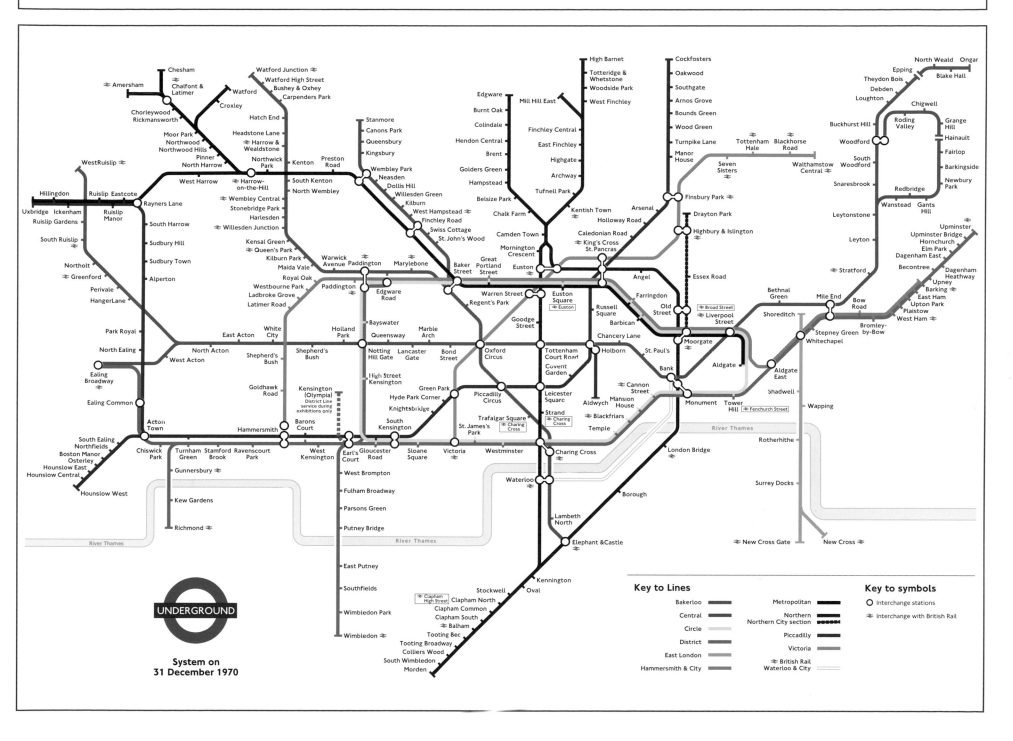

UNDERGROUND

**System on
31 December 1970**

Key to Lines

Bakerloo	Metropolitan	
Central	Northern	
Circle	Northern City section	
District	Piccadilly	
East London	Victoria	
Hammersmith & City	British Rail	
	Waterloo & City	

Key to symbols

◯ Interchange stations

⇌ Interchange with British Rail

Principal developments of the decade

Right Green Park on the Jubilee Line, opened in 1979.

Bakerloo Line

1979 Stanmore to Baker Street branch transferred to the new Jubilee Line on 1 May.

Piccadilly Line

1971 Building began on the 5.6km (3½ mile) extension from Hounslow West to Heathrow Airport, with an intermediate station at Hatton Cross, in April 1971.

1975 Hatton Cross opened on 19 July.

1977 London Airport was connected by tube to central London with the opening of Heathrow Central on 16 December.

Metropolitan Line

1971 The Underground's steam locomotives, used for the haulage of engineers' trains, were withdrawn, followed by a commemorative run from Barbican to Neasden depot on 6 June.

Victoria Line

1971 The extension southwards from Victoria to Brixton opened, together with intermediate stations at Vauxhall and Stockwell, on 23 July.

1972 Pimlico Station, for the Tate Gallery, opened on 14 September.

Jubilee Line

1972 Work commenced on the first stage of tunnelling of what was originally called the Fleet Line, between Baker Street and Charing Cross.

1977 The name was changed to Jubilee Line to mark the Silver Jubilee of the accession to the throne of Queen Elizabeth II in 1952.

1979 The line between Stanmore and Baker Street (formerly part of the Bakerloo Line and originally operated by the Metropolitan Railway) and the new tunnel section to Charing Cross, was opened by HRH the Prince of Wales on 30 April 1979 and to the public the following day.

Northern Line – Northern City section

1975 Tube rolling stock ran for the last time on 4 October, in preparation for the line's transfer to British Rail and its re-conversion to take main line size trains.

Opening dates of stations, name changes and closures

Stations opened or first served by Underground trains

23.07.1971	Brixton	VICTORIA LINE
23.07.1971	Vauxhall	VICTORIA LINE
23.07.1971	Stockwell	VICTORIA LINE
14.09.1972	Pimlico	VICTORIA LINE
19.07.1975	Hatton Cross	PICCADILLY LINE
16.12.1977	Heathrow Central	PICCADILLY LINE *now Heathrow T123*
1.05.1979	Baker Street	JUBILEE LINE
1.05.1979	Bond Street	JUBILEE LINE
1.05.1979	Charing Cross	JUBILEE LINE
1.05.1979	Charing Cross	NORTHERN LINE *re-built from Strand*
1.05.1979	Green Park	JUBILEE LINE

Station names changed

	from	*to*
c.1974	Chorley Wood	Chorleywood
6.05.1974	Bushey & Oxhey	Bushey
4.08.1974	Charing Cross	Charing Cross Embankment
20.07.1976	Brent	Brent Cross
12.09.1976	Charing Cross Embankment	Embankment
1.05.1979	Trafalgar Square BAKERLOO LINE	Charing Cross for Trafalgar Square
1.05.1979	Strand NORTHERN LINE	Charing Cross

Stations last served by Underground trains

16.06.1973	Strand	NORTHERN LINE
6.09.1975	Moorgate	NORTHERN CITY *transferred to BR*
3.10.1975	Essex Road	NORTHERN CITY *transferred to BR*
4.10.1975	Drayton Park	NORTHERN CITY *transferred to BR*
4.10.1975	Highbury & Islington	NORTHERN CITY *transferred to BR*
4.10.1975	Old Street	NORTHERN CITY *transferred to BR*

Right Work proceeded on the airport extension during the 1970s, resulting in re-sited platforms at Hounslow West and completely new stations at Hatton Cross and the terminus, shown here, Heathrow Central.

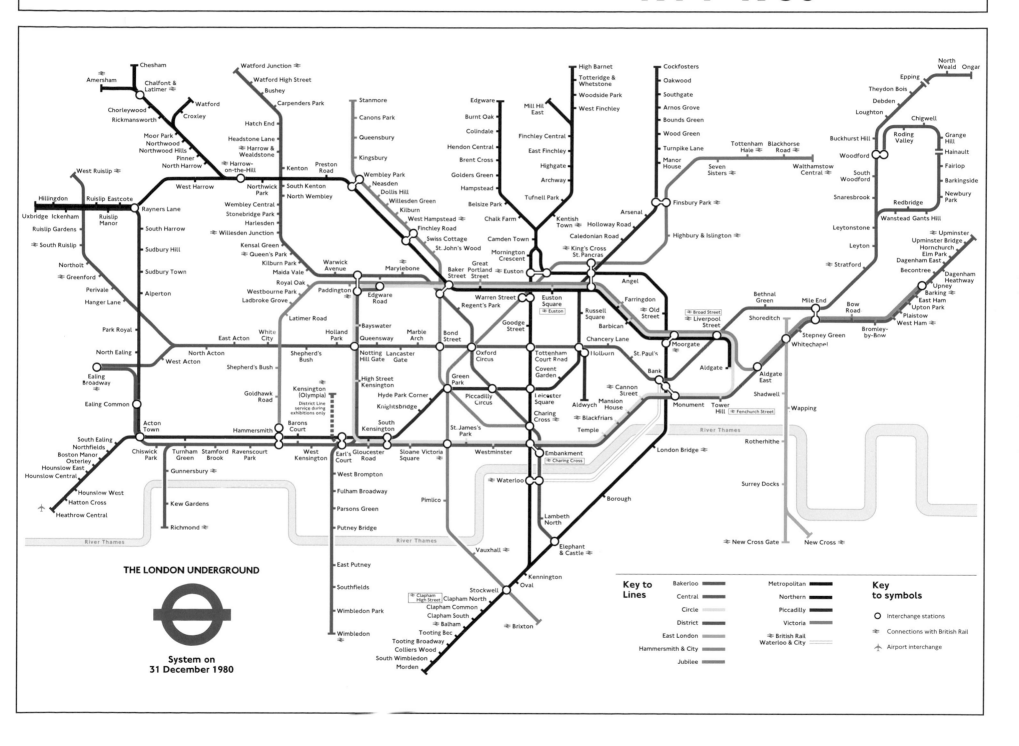

THE LONDON UNDERGROUND

**System on
31 December 1980**

Key to Lines			
Bakerloo		Metropolitan	
Central		Northern	
Circle		Piccadilly	
District		Victoria	
East London		British Rail Waterloo & City	
Hammersmith & City			
Jubilee			

Key to symbols

O Interchange stations

⇌ Connections with British Rail

✈ Airport interchange

Kensington (Olympia) District Line service during exhibitions only

27

Exterior and interior views of the Jubilee Line 1983 Stock. The fleet of trains was scrapped after only 16 years, when replaced by entirely new stock built for the opening of the extension to Stratford in 1999. The use of single-leaf doors followed those installed on the District Line D78 Stock, but were a cause of congestion on the smaller tube stock. Flat fronts to the driving cars lacked the finesse of traditional bow fronts. On the credit side, the cars had very spacious looking interiors, decorated in yellow and orange. They were also the first Underground trains to be controlled with the aid of computer chips.

Principal developments of the decade

Right 'Art on the Underground' was a new series of posters, evolved in the 1980s.

Centre right A test train on the Docklands Light Railway, shortly before it was opened to the public on 31 August 1987.

Below Zonal fares were introduced on a small scale in 1981 with flat fares within a west-central zone and an east-central zone. This system was enlarged in 1983 to cover the entire London Transport bus and Underground networks within the Greater London area, extending outwards in five concentric circles from a single central zone.

Bakerloo Line

1982 Trains withdrawn between Stonebridge Park and Watford Junction, leaving British Rail in total charge of providing the service, on 24 September.

1984 Tube trains were re-instated between Stonebridge Park and Harrow & Wealdstone on 4 June.

The new Kew by Tube
The Princess of Wales Conservatory. Nearest station Kew Gardens

Piccadilly Line

1986 A single-line loop from Hatton Cross to the existing Heathrow Central was constructed underground, with an intermediate station serving Terminal 4 opened on 12 April.

One-person operation

1984 Circle and Hammersmith & City C Stock are the first trains to be converted to one-person operation by abolishing the guard and handing over door operation to the driver.

Docklands Light Railway

1987 The two branches from Tower Gateway and Stratford, both terminating at Island Gardens, opened on 31 August 1987.

Opening dates of stations, name changes and closures

Stations opened or first served by Underground trains

4.06.1984	Harrow & Wealdstone [BR]	BAKERLOO LINE *re-served*
4.06.1984	Kenton [BR]	BAKERLOO LINE *re-served*
4.06.1984	North Wembley [BR]	BAKERLOO LINE *re-served*
4.06.1984	South Kenton [BR]	BAKERLOO LINE *re-served*
4.06.1984	Wembley Central [BR]	BAKERLOO LINE *re-served*
7.04.1986	Kensington (Olympia)	DISTRICT LINE *regular service*
12.04.1986	Heathrow Terminal 4	PICCADILLY LINE

Stations opened on the Docklands Light Railway

31.08.1987	All Saints
31.08.1987	Bow Church
31.08.1987	Crossharbour
31.08.1987	Devons Road
31.08.1987	Heron Quays
31.08.1987	Island Gardens
31.08.1987	Shadwell
31.08.1987	Limehouse
31.08.1987	Mudchute *first site*
31.08.1987	Poplar
31.08.1987	South Quay
31.08.1987	Tower Gateway
31.08.1987	Westferry
31.08.1987	West India Quay

Station names changed

	from	*to*
3.09.1983	Heathrow Central	Heathrow Central Terminals 1,2,3
12.04.1986	Heathrow Central Terminals 1,2,3	Heathrow Terminals 1,2,3
24.10.1989	Surrey Docks	Surrey Quays

Stations last served by Underground trains

31.10.1981	Blake Hall	CENTRAL LINE
24.09.1982	Bushey [BR]	BAKERLOO *retains BR service*
24.09.1982	Carpenders Park [BR]	BAKERLOO *retains BR service*
24.09.1982	Harrow & Wealdstone [BR]	BAKERLOO *retains BR service*
24.09.1982	Hatch End [BR]	BAKERLOO *retains BR service*
24.09.1982	Headstone Lane [BR]	BAKERLOO *retains BR service*
24.09.1982	Kenton [BR]	BAKERLOO *retains BR service*
24.09.1982	South Kenton [BR]	BAKERLOO *retains BR service*
24.09.1982	North Wembley [BR]	BAKERLOO *retains BR service*
24.09.1982	Watford High Street [BR]	BAKERLOO *retains BR service*
24.09.1982	Watford Junction [BR]	BAKERLOO *retains BR service*
24.09.1982	Wembley Central [BR]	BAKERLOO *retains BR service*

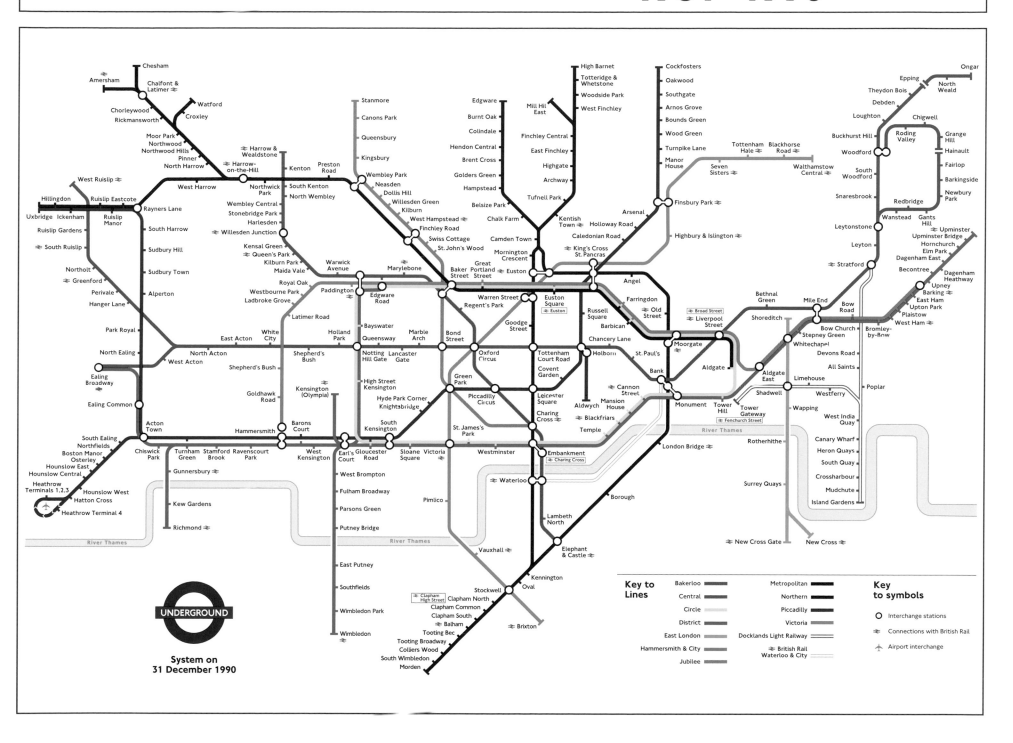

System on
31 December 1990

Key to Lines		
Bakerloo	Metropolitan	
Central	Northern	
Circle	Piccadilly	
District	Victoria	
East London	Docklands Light Railway	
Hammersmith & City	British Rail Waterloo & City	
Jubilee		

Key to symbols

○ Interchange stations

⇌ Connections with British Rail

✈ Airport interchange

Principal developments of the decade

Central Line

1994 North Weald and Ongar stations closed when the passenger train service was withdrawn from the single-line Epping to Ongar branch on 30 September.

Jubilee Line

1999 First part of the extension opened between the new terminus at Stratford and North Greenwich on 14 May; to Bermondsey on 17 September; to Waterloo on 24 September and connected with the original line south of Green Park on 20 November – the link with Charing Cross having closed the day before.

Northern Line

1992 Mornington Crescent closed 23 October until 1998.

Piccadilly Line

1994 Aldwych branch closed on 30 September.

Waterloo & City Line

1994 Ownership was transferred from British Rail to London Underground on 1 April and operation from 5 April.

Docklands Light Railway

1991 The branch to Bank opened on 29 January.

1994 The Poplar to Beckton line opened on 28 March.

1995 The link between Poplar and Westferry was brought into use on 31 July.

1999 The section under the River Thames to Greenwich and Lewisham opened on 20 November.

Opening dates of stations, name changes and closures

Stations opened or first served by Underground trains

Date	Station	Line
5.04.1994	Bank	WATERLOO & CITY LINE
5.04.1994	Waterloo	WATERLOO & CITY LINE
14.05.1999	Canning Town	JUBILEE LINE
14.05.1999	North Greenwich	JUBILEE LINE
14.05.1999	Stratford	JUBILEE LINE
14.05.1999	West Ham	JUBILEE LINE
19.08.1999	Canada Water	EAST LONDON LINE
17.09.1999	Bermondsey	JUBILEE LINE
17.09.1999	Canada Water	JUBILEE LINE
17.09.1999	Canary Wharf	JUBILEE LINE
24.09.1999	Waterloo	JUBILEE LINE
7.10.1999	London Bridge	JUBILEE LINE
20.11.1999	Southwark	JUBILEE LINE
22.12.1999	Westminster	JUBILEE LINE

Stations opened or first served by DLR trains

29.01.1991	Bank
28.03.1994	Beckton
28.03.1994	Beckton Park
28.03.1994	Blackwall
28.03.1994	Custom House
28.03.1994	Cyprus
28.03.1994	East India
28.03.1994	Prince Regent
28.03.1994	Royal Albert
28.03.1994	Royal Victoria
28.11.1994	Gallions Reach
15.01.1996	Pudding Mill Lane
20.11.1999	Elverson Road
20.11.1999	Greenwich
20.11.1999	Lewisham
20.11.1999	Mudchute *re-sited*
20.11.1999	Island Gardens *re-sited*

Station names changed

	from	to
14.08.1995	Crossharbour	Crossharbour & London Arena

Stations last served by Underground or DLR trains

Date	Station	Line
30.09.1994	Aldwych	PICCADILLY LINE
30.09.1994	North Weald	CENTRAL LINE
30.09.1994	Ongar	CENTRAL LINE
19.11.1999	Charing Cross	JUBILEE LINE

Two of the impressive stations built for the Jubilee Line extension to Stratford are Canary Wharf *above* and North Greenwich *right*.

Far right The last train on the Central Line's very rural Ongar branch stops for photographs at North Weald.

1991–2000

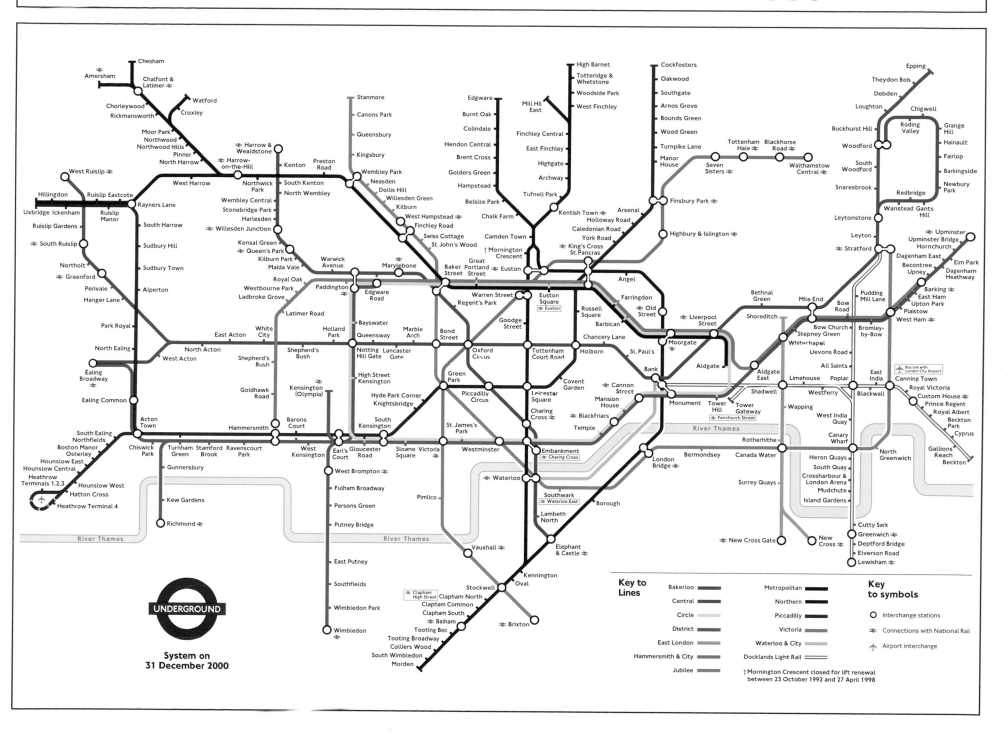

Key to Lines

Bakerloo		Metropolitan
Central		Northern
Circle		Piccadilly
District		Victoria
East London		Waterloo & City
Hammersmith & City		Docklands Light Rail
Jubilee		

Key to symbols

○ Interchange stations
⇌ Connections with National Rail
✈ Airport interchange

† Mornington Crescent closed for lift renewal between 23 October 1992 and 27 April 1998

UNDERGROUND

System on 31 December 2000

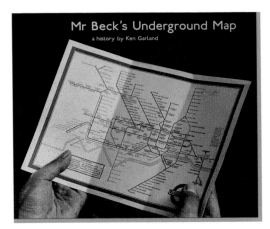

Mr Beck's Underground Map *Ken Garland*

A suggestion in 1931 by a junior draughtsman, Harry Beck, for a different approach to mapping its railways using an easy-to-follow diagrammatic method based on straight lines, was liked by the public, though no-one has ever attempted to measure its commercial value to the Underground. The map's successors are still with Londoners today and its principles have been used in many other cities and countries.

185414 168 6   Hardback. Colour throughout.
80 pages 240 by 275 mm.   **£12.95**

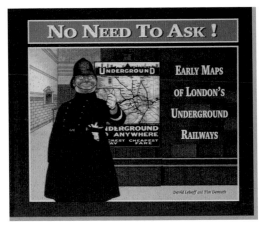

No Need to Ask! *David Leboff and Tim Demuth*

This companion volume to Mr Beck's Underground Map traces the large range of geographically based maps issued by the companies to promote their rapidly developing Underground system.

185414 215 1   Hardback. Colour throughout.
80 pages 240 by 275 mm.   **£12.95**

Pleasure Trips by Underground
Jonathan Riddell

With the majority of its passengers travelling during the weekday rush hours, the Underground has long recognised the benefits of promoting leisure travel on its lines. Top poster artists were commissioned to encourage people to travel by Underground to the London stores, open spaces, the River, evening entertainment and sporting and ceremonial events.

This book celebrates the work of these artists and shows how the Underground sought to get its message across to Londoners to make their pleasure trips by Underground.

185414 200 3   Hardback. Full colour throughout.
96 pages 240 by 275 mm.   **£14.95**

The Story of London's Underground

John R. Day and John Reed

This book covers all the major developments on the London Underground and many of the less significant, but fascinating, aspects of its history. The extensive research that has gone into the text of this new edition has also been applied to the illustrations and all known sources of Underground material have been tapped.

185414 245 3   Hardback. Illustrated in colour and black and white.
216 pages. 273 by 210 mm.
£25.00

Available from

Capital Transport

PO Box 250, Harrow, HA3 5ZH.